D0190501

ALL I GOT FOR
CHRISTMAS
WAS THIS
LOUSY
JOKE
BOOK

ALL I GOT FOR

CHRISTMAS
WAS THIS
LOUSY
JOKE
BOOK

NICK HARRIS

Michael O'Mara Books Limited

First published in Great Britain in 2011 as *A Dyslexic Walks Into A Bra ...*
This new edition first published in Great Britain in 2017 by
Michael O'Mara Books Limited
9 Lion Yard
Tremadoc Road
London SW4 7NQ

Copyright © Michael O'Mara Books Limited 2017

All rights reserved. No part of this publication may be reproduced, stored in a retrieval system, or transmitted by any means, without the prior permission in writing of the publisher, nor be otherwise circulated in any form of binding or cover other than that in which it is published and without a similar condition including this condition being imposed on the subsequent purchaser.

A CIP catalogue record for this book is available from the British Library.

Papers used by Michael O'Mara Books Limited are natural, recyclable products made from wood grown in sustainable forests. The manufacturing processes conform to the environmental regulations of the country of origin.

ISBN: 978-1-78243-881-6

1 2 3 4 5 6 7 8 9 10

www.mombooks.com

Cover design and title page illustration by Andrew Pinder

Designed and typeset by Design 23

Printed and bound by CPI Group (UK) Ltd, Croydon, CR0 4YY

Contents

Introduction

Jokes have been around ever since the day the doctor told Moses to keep taking the tablets. The Romans enjoyed nothing more than a good Persian joke, no doubt Henry VIII had a nice line in marriage jokes – it was probably wise to laugh at them in any case – and even Queen Victoria must occasionally have found something to amuse her. So in the belief that a day without laughter is a day wasted, I have compiled this bumper book of jokes for all ages, including long jokes, one-liners, funny lists and excruciating puns on a wide variety of subjects ranging from school to sex, money to music, and doctors to drunks.

Telling jokes will never go out of fashion. With the possible exception of a papal blessing, it is hard to imagine any occasion that would not be enhanced by a good joke. As Woody Allen so memorably put it: 'I am thankful for laughter, except when milk comes out of my nose.'

Adam and Eve

One day, the Lord said to Adam: 'It's time for you and Eve to begin the process of populating Earth, so I want you to kiss her.'

'Yes, Lord,' said Adam, 'but what is a kiss?'

So the Lord gave a brief description of a kiss to Adam who took Eve by the hand and led her to a nearby bush. A few minutes later, Adam emerged and said: 'Thank you, Lord. That was most enjoyable.'

'I thought you might like it,' said the Lord, 'so now I want you to caress Eve.'

'Certainly, Lord,' replied Adam. 'But what is a caress?'

Again the Lord gave a brief description to Adam

who went back behind the bush with Eve. Fifteen minutes later, Adam returned smiling: 'Thank you, Lord. That was even better than the kiss.'

'Good,' said the Lord. 'You have done well, Adam, and now I want you to make love to Eve.'

Adam asked: 'What is "make love", Lord?'

So the Lord gave Adam directions, and Adam went behind the bush with Eve. This time he reappeared just a few seconds later and asked: 'Lord, what is a headache?'

God had almost finished creating the universe when he realized he still had a couple of items left over in his bag of creations. So he stopped by to visit Adam and Eve in the Garden of Eden.

'Listen,' said God, 'one of the items I can give away is the ability to stand up and pee. It might not sound very exciting, but it could be useful. So do either of you want it?'

'Me, me, me!' pleaded Adam, jumping up and down excitedly. 'I want to be able to pee standing up. Please, God, give it to me.'

'Is that okay with you, Eve?' asked God.

'Sure,' said Eve wearily. 'If it keeps him happy, let him have it.'

'Very well,' said God. 'From now on, Adam, you

will be able to pee standing up. Right, now what else is left in the bag? Oh, yes. Multiple orgasms . . .'

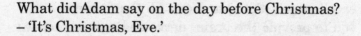

What did Adam say on the day before Christmas?
– 'It's Christmas, Eve.'

A feminist speaker was addressing a large group and asked: 'Where would Man be today if it were not for Woman?'

She paused for a moment and looked around the room before saying: 'I repeat, where would Man be today if it were not for Woman?'

From the back of the room, a lone male voice called out: 'He'd be in the Garden of Eden eating strawberries.'

One day, God decided to make a companion for Adam. He told St Peter of his decision, adding that he wanted to make a being who was similar to Man, yet was different – someone who could offer Man comfort, companionship and pleasure. God said he intended calling this being Woman. So St Peter set about creating this being and thought of ways in which she would be appealing and could provide physical pleasure to Man. When he had finished, he showed God his ideas.

God was mightily impressed. 'You have done an excellent job, Peter, and now all that remains is for you to provide the brain, nerve endings and senses to Woman.'

'I could actually use your help on this, Lord,' said St Peter. 'Have you had any thoughts about how you want Woman to behave?'

'Yes,' replied God. 'I want you to make her brain slightly smaller, yet more intuitive, more feeling, more compassionate, and more adaptable than Man's.'

'How many nerve endings shall I put in her hands?' asked St Peter.

'How many did we put in Adam's?'

'Seventeen thousand.'

'Then we shall do the same for Woman.'

'And how many nerve endings shall we put in her feet?'

'How many did we put in Adam's?'

'Seven thousand two hundred.'

'Ah yes, that was because these beings are constantly on their feet, so they benefit from having fewer nerve endings there. Do the same for Woman.'

'How many nerve endings shall we put in Woman's genitals?' asked St Peter.

'How many did we put in Adam's?'

'Five hundred and twenty.'

'Yes, we did want Adam to have a means of receiving extra pleasure in life, didn't we? Do the same for Woman.'

'Certainly, Lord.'

'No, wait,' said God. 'Give her ten thousand – I want her to scream out my name!'

Why Eve Was Created

God knew Adam would never go out and buy a new fig leaf when his was worn out and would therefore need Eve to buy one for him.

God was concerned that Adam would get lost in the Garden of Eden and would not ask for directions.

As the Keeper of the Garden, Adam would never remember where he had left his tools.

God knew that Adam would be incapable of making a doctor's or dentist's appointment for himself.

God knew that Adam would never remember which night to put the garbage out for collection.

God knew that one day Adam would need someone to locate and hand him the remote.

Adam was walking round the Garden of Eden, feeling sad and lonely. He complained to God that he had nobody to talk to.

God said: 'I was thinking about giving you a companion called Woman. This person will cook for you and wash your clothes. She will agree with whatever you say. She will bear your children without complaint and will never ask you to get up in the middle of the night to help with the care. She will never nag you and will always admit when she is in the wrong. She will never bear a grudge and will dress to please you. She will give you love whenever you want it.'

'Wow!' exclaimed Adam. 'How much would a woman like that cost me?'

'An arm and a leg,' replied God.

Adam said: 'What can I get for a rib . . . ?'

Contrary to popular belief, it was apparently Eve who was created first. And after a month in the Garden of Eden, she was visited by God.

'How are things?' asked God.

'Everything is wonderful,' said Eve, 'except for these three breasts you have given me. The middle one pushes out the other two and keeps getting caught on branches. I feel as if it's always in the way.'

'That's a fair point,' said God, 'but give me a break, it was my first attempt at this creation game. I gave the animals six, so I figured half would be about right for you. But I see what you mean, so I'll fix it right away.'

And God reached down, tore out Eve's middle breast and lobbed it into some bushes.

A month later, God visited Eve again. 'How is my favourite creation?' he asked.

'Yes, fine,' replied Eve, 'but I think you may have made an oversight. You see, all the animals are paired off. The ewe has her ram, the cow has her bull – in fact all the animals have a mate except me. I'm starting to feel lonely.'

'You're right,' said God. 'Silly me! You do need a mate, so I shall immediately create Man from a part of your body. Now, let's see . . . where did I put that useless tit?'

Animals

An elephant was walking through the jungle, but with each step he took he trampled dozens of ants under his huge feet. The ants became so angry that they started crawling up the elephant's body, hell-bent on revenge.

As the elephant felt their presence on his skin, he shook his body, causing all of the ants except one to plunge to the ground. This one ant clung on bravely to the elephant's neck while all the ants on the ground started to yell: 'Strangle him! Strangle him!'

Two sheep were standing in a field. One went: 'Baaaaa.'

The other went: 'Damn! I was going to say that.'

One afternoon in the Arctic, a father polar bear and his polar bear son were sitting in the snow. The cub turned to his father and said: 'Dad, am I one hundred per cent polar bear?'

'Of course, son,' replied the father. 'You are one hundred per cent polar bear.'

A few minutes later, the cub turned to his father again and said: 'Dad, tell me the truth, I can take it. Am I one hundred per cent polar bear? No brown bear or black bear or grizzly bear?'

The father put a loving paw on his son's head. 'Son,' he said, 'I am one hundred per cent polar bear, your mother is one hundred per cent polar bear, so you are definitely one hundred per cent polar bear.'

The cub seemed satisfied, but a few minutes later he turned to his father once more and said: 'Look, Dad, I don't want you saying things just to spare my feelings. I have to know: am I one hundred per cent polar bear?'

By now the father was becoming distressed by the continual questioning and said: 'Why do you keep asking if you are one hundred per cent polar bear?'

The cub replied: 'Because I'm freezing!'

Two dog owners were discussing the intelligence of their pets.

'The smartest dog I ever had', said the first, 'was a Jack Russell that could play cards. He was brilliant at poker – he could even beat professionals. But I had to have him put down.'

'You had him put to sleep?' said the other. 'You must be crazy. A bright dog like that could be worth a million dollars!'

'I had no choice. I caught him using marked cards.'

What has four legs and flies?
– A dead horse.

In the jungle, two monkeys were sitting in a tree beneath which a lion was sleeping peacefully. One monkey said to the other: 'I dare you to go down there and kick that lion in the butt!'

'Okay,' said the other monkey, feeling brave, 'I'll do it.'

So he ran down the tree, kicked the lion as hard as he could in the butt, and then escaped by running off through the jungle. Roused from his slumbers, the angry lion immediately gave chase and was soon gaining fast on the monkey until he was only about fifty yards behind him. Realizing he had to act quickly to avoid being eaten by the lion, the monkey picked up a newspaper that was lying on the ground and sat on a tree stump pretending to read it.

A few moments later, the lion arrived on the scene. 'Did you see a monkey pass this way just now?' asked the lion.

The monkey replied: 'Do you mean the one that kicked the lion in the butt?'

The lion groaned: 'Don't tell me it's in the papers already!'

A woman went to the veterinary clinic to collect her sick dog. The vet came in carrying the dog and said: 'I'm really sorry, but I'm going to have to put your dog down.'

'Why?' sobbed the woman.

'Because he's too heavy.'

In the middle of the night two bats were hanging upside down in their cave. The first bat turned to the second bat and said: 'Do you fancy going out to get some nice tasty blood for a late-night snack?'

'Where are we going to find blood at this time of night?' asked the second bat.

'Okay,' said the first bat. 'I'll fly off by myself.'

Twenty minutes later, the first bat returned to the cave with blood dripping from his mouth and running all over his body.

'Wow!' exclaimed the second bat. 'Where did you get all that blood?'

'See that tree over there?' said the first bat.

'Yes.'

'Well I didn't!'

When Noah lowered the ramp of the Ark for all the animals to leave, he ordered them: 'Go forth and multiply.'

All the animals left except for two snakes which remained curled up in the corner of the Ark.

'Why will you not go forth and multiply?' demanded Noah.

'We can't,' said the snakes. 'We're adders.'

Did you hear about the dog that loved eating garlic?
– His bark was much worse than his bite.

An elderly snake went to an optician and said: 'My eyesight has got so bad that I can't see to hunt anymore. I think I might need a pair of glasses.'

So the optician fixed the snake up with a pair of glasses and told him to come back if he still couldn't see properly.

Two weeks later, the snake was back at the optician's. 'I'm depressed,' he complained.

'Why, what's the problem?' asked the optician. 'Haven't the glasses helped?'

'The glasses are fine,' sighed the snake. 'But I've realized that I've been living with a garden hose for the past five years!'

Two fleas left a restaurant. Outside, one turned to the other and said: 'Do you want to walk or take a dog?'

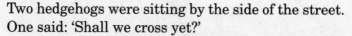

Two hedgehogs were sitting by the side of the street. One said: 'Shall we cross yet?'

'No way,' said the other hedgehog. 'Look what happened to the zebra!'

A zookeeper needed some extra animals for his zoo, so he decided to write a letter. But unfortunately he didn't know the plural of 'mongoose'.

He started the letter: 'Dear Sir, I need two mongeese.' But that didn't sound right, so he tried again. 'Dear Sir, I need two mongooses.' But that didn't sound right either. Then he had an idea. 'Dear Sir, I need a mongoose, and while you're at it, send me another one.'

Two female rhinoceroses at the zoo were eagerly awaiting the arrival of a new male. When he was led into the paddock, they quickly went over and introduced themselves.

'Hi,' said one, 'I'm Sharon and this is my friend Linda.'

'Hi,' said the male. 'My name's Neil.'

'Ooooh!' they trilled. 'Not *the* rhino Neil?'

A tomcat and a female cat were getting amorous in the back yard one night. Eventually he purred into her ear: 'I'd die for you.'

With wide eyes, she answered: 'How many times?'

What's the difference between a businessman and a warm dog?
– The businessman wears a suit, the dog just pants.

A man was passing a pet shop when he saw a talking monkey advertised for sale. He was so impressed by its extensive vocabulary that he bought it on the spot.

That evening he took it to his local bar and bet everyone twenty dollars that the monkey could talk. Nine people accepted the challenge but despite its new owner's coaxing and prompting, the monkey refused to say a word and the man had to pay up. When he got it home, the man was puzzled to hear the monkey talking freely.

The next evening, the man returned to the bar and bet everyone thirty dollars that the monkey could talk. Again there were plenty of takers but, to the man's fury, the monkey remained silent. After paying up, the man took the monkey outside.

'I'm taking you back to the shop,' he raged. 'You're

a complete waste of money!'

'Calm down,' said the monkey. 'Think of the odds we'll get tomorrow.'

Why do brown bears have fur coats?
– Because they'd look silly in anoraks.

A Jack Russell terrier went to the job centre. He said to the clerk: 'I'm looking for work.'

'Amazing!' said the clerk. 'A talking dog! I'll fix you up with a job in no time.'

After making a quick phone call, the clerk handed the dog a piece of paper and said: 'There you go. You start at the circus on Monday.'

'That's no use to me,' protested the dog. 'I'm a plumber.'

A US tourist guide was addressing a group of holidaymakers about the dangers of hiking in grizzly bear territory. He warned: 'Most encounters occur when hikers, being extra quiet along the trails in the hope of viewing wildlife, unexpectedly stumble upon bears. The surprise can be disastrous. To avoid this, we recommend that hikers wear tiny bells on their clothing to warn the bears of their presence. Finally, you should exercise caution when you spot telltale signs of bears in the area, particularly if you see bear droppings.'

One tourist asked: 'How do you identify bear droppings?'

'Easy,' explained the guide. 'They're the ones with all the tiny bells in them!'

An adult hedgehog was teaching two young hedgehogs how to cross the road without getting killed. He said: 'If you're in the middle of the road when a car comes along, just curl up into a ball and the vehicle's wheels will pass harmlessly either side of you. It's simple.'

To illustrate his point, the adult hedgehog then walked out into the middle of the road and as soon as a car appeared, he curled up into a ball. Just as he had predicted, the car's wheels passed by, leaving him unscathed.

Next, one of the younger hedgehogs tried it. He walked into the path of an oncoming car, curled up into a ball, and the car's wheels passed by, leaving him undamaged.

Finally the third hedgehog had a go. He walked to the centre of the road and curled up into a ball as a car approached. The car passed over it and squashed the hedgehog flat.

'What did he do wrong?' cried the second hedgehog.

'Nothing,' said the adult hedgehog. 'He was just unlucky that a Reliant Robin came along.'

An explorer in the jungle saw a monkey with a tin opener. He called out to the monkey: 'You don't need a tin opener to peel a banana.'

'I know,' replied the monkey. 'I'm not stupid. This is for the custard.'

The zoo owner told the new keeper: 'You idiot! You left the door of the lions' cage open all night!'

'What's the problem?' said the keeper. 'Who's going to steal a lion?'

A keen duck hunter was looking to buy a new bird dog. His search ended when he found a dog that was able to walk on water in order to retrieve a duck. Amazed by his discovery, he was sure none of his friends would ever believe him.

He decided to try and break the news to a friend, an eternal pessimist who was never impressed by anything. In the hope that even he would be impressed by a dog that could walk on water, the pessimist was invited to join the hunter and his dog on a trip to the country. However the hunter deliberately refrained from mentioning the dog's special talent – he wanted his friend to see for himself.

The two men and the dog made their way to a good hunting lake and as they waited by the shore, a flock of ducks flew overhead. The men fired, and a duck fell. The dog responded and jumped into the water, but instead of sinking, it walked across the water to retrieve the bird, never getting more than its paws wet. This continued throughout the day. Each time a duck fell, the dog walked across the surface of the water to retrieve it.

The pessimist carefully watched everything, but did not say a word. Then on the drive home, the hunter casually asked his friend: 'Did you notice anything unusual about my new dog?'

'I certainly did,' replied the pessimist. 'He can't swim.'

What kind of monkey can fly?
– A hot air baboon.

Two dog owners were talking in the park. One said:
'I'm sick of my dog. The trouble is he'll chase anyone
on a bike.'

'What are you going to do?' asked the other. 'Have
him put down?'

'No, I think I'll just take his bike away.'

Things You Can Learn From Your Dog

When loved ones come home, always run to greet
them.

When it's in your best interest, practise obedience.
Let others know when they've invaded your
territory.

Never pass up the opportunity to go for a joyride.

Enjoy the experience of fresh air and the wind in
your face.

Take naps and stretch before rising.

Avoid biting when a simple growl will do.

Delight in the simple joy of a long walk.

On hot days, drink lots of water and lie under a shady tree.

Eat with gusto and enthusiasm, but stop when you have had enough.

When someone is having a bad day, be silent, sit close by and nuzzle them gently.

If what you want lies buried, dig until you find it.

Two slugs were slithering along the pavement. As they rounded a corner, they found themselves stuck behind two snails.
   'Oh, no!' groaned one of the slugs. 'Caravans!'

What's worse than a bull in a china shop?
– A hedgehog in a condom factory.

29

A zoo had acquired a rare species of gorilla but although the female was in season, they had no male gorilla to mate with her. In desperation they asked one of the keepers whether he would be willing to have sex with the gorilla for five hundred dollars. The keeper asked for a little time to think about the idea.

The following morning, he went back to the zoo bosses with his answer. 'I'll agree to have sex with the gorilla,' he said, 'but on three conditions. First, I don't want to have to kiss her. Second, I want nothing to do with any offspring that may result from this union.'

'Yes, that's all fine,' said the zoo bosses. 'What is your third condition?'

The keeper said: 'You'll have to give me another week to come up with the five hundred bucks.'

A man hated his wife's cat so much that he decided to get rid of it by driving it twenty blocks from home and dumping it. But as he returned home, he saw the cat wandering up the driveway.

So he drove the cat thirty blocks away and dumped it, but when he arrived back home, the cat was waiting for him on the front step.

In desperation he drove the cat fifty miles out into the country and left it in the middle of a forest.

Four hours later, his wife answered the phone at

home. It was her husband. 'Honey,' he asked, 'is the cat there?'

'Yes,' said the wife. 'Why?'

'Just put him on the line, please. I need directions.'

A woman saw a newspaper advert that offered a pure-bred police dog for sale for twenty-five dollars. Thinking it a bargain, she rang the number and bought the dog. But when the owner delivered it, she found that she had bought nothing but a mangy-looking mongrel.

She told the owner: 'How can you possibly call that scruffy mutt a pure-bred police dog?'

'Don't let his looks deceive you,' said the owner. 'He's working undercover.'

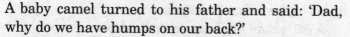

A baby camel turned to his father and said: 'Dad, why do we have humps on our back?'

'Well, son,' replied the father, 'our humps contain the fat needed to sustain us through all the days when we're out in the desert.'

'Oh, right,' said the baby camel. 'Dad, why do we have long eyelashes?'

'They're to protect our eyes from the sandstorms that rage in the desert.'

'I understand. Dad, why do we have big padded feet?'

'Because the sand in the desert is very soft and we need big feet so that we can walk on the sand without sinking.'

'Thanks, Dad. I get it now. Just one more question: what are we doing in the city zoo?'

Why aren't dogs good dancers?
– Because they've got two left feet.

A man was driving along the road when a cat ran out in front of his car. Unable to stop in time, he ran over the cat and killed it. Feeling guilty, he looked at the address on the cat's collar and set off to relay the sad news to the animal's owner.

A little old lady answered the door.

'I'm very sorry,' said the man, 'but I'm afraid I've run over your cat. I'd like to replace it.'

'Sure,' said the old lady. 'How are you at catching mice?'

A cash-strapped zoo was desperate for a major attraction to boost falling visitor numbers. Unable to afford any new animals, the zoo manager persuaded a visitor to dress up in a gorilla costume and masquerade as a great ape.

The deception worked well as the man threw himself into the role with great enthusiasm, devouring buckets of bananas, swinging from branches, prowling his cage menacingly and beating his chest with vigour. But then one day, he went too far and accidentally fell into the lion enclosure next door.

'Help! Help!' cried the bogus gorilla.

The lion let out a tremendous roar, then rushed at him, put his paw on the gorilla's chest and growled: 'Shut up, or we'll both lose our jobs!'

An explorer in the African jungle heard about a plan to capture the legendary King Kong. And sure enough when he came to a clearing there before him, imprisoned in a cage, sat the imposing figure of King Kong.

It occurred to the explorer that he could be the first person ever to touch the great ape and so tentatively he inched towards the cage. Since King

Kong appeared quite passive, the explorer thought he would take a chance and reach through the bars to touch him. But as soon as he made contact with the gorilla's fur, King Kong went berserk. He immediately rose to his feet, began beating his chest and with an awesome display of strength, burst through the bars of his cage.

As the explorer ran for his life, King Kong set off in hot pursuit. Instinctively the explorer headed for the heart of the jungle, hoping that he might be able to hide from his manic pursuer, but wherever he tried to conceal himself, King Kong always managed to find him.

As night began to fall, the explorer prayed that he would be able to lose the gorilla in the darkness but no matter how fast he ran, the sound of King Kong's pounding footsteps was only ever about fifty yards behind.

For three long days and nights, the explorer ran through Africa with King Kong always close behind, occasionally letting out a menacing roar from his vast throat. Eventually the explorer reached the west coast. There were no ships in sight for an easy escape, so he realized the only option was to dive into the sea and hope that King Kong couldn't swim. But to his horror, the gorilla jumped in straight after him and demonstrated an excellent front crawl.

On and on they swam across the Atlantic – rarely separated by more than thirty yards – until four months later the weary explorer arrived in Brazil. He scrambled ashore with as much energy as he could muster, only to see the mighty King Kong right behind him, still beating his chest ferociously and with steam billowing from his nostrils. Through the streets of Rio they stumbled, explorer and ape equally exhausted, until the explorer took a wrong turn and ended up down a dead end, his escape barred by a twenty-foot-high wall.

With nowhere left to run, he sank to his knees in despair and pleaded to King Kong: 'Do whatever you want with me. Kill me, eat me, do what you like, but make it quick. Just put me out of my misery.'

King Kong slowly stalked over to the cowering explorer, prodded him with a giant paw and bellowed with a terrifying roar: 'You're it!'

Army, Navy and Air Force

An army sergeant was appalled to discover that ten of his men were late back to camp following leave. As he waited impatiently at the barracks gates, one man finally ran up to him, panting heavily.

'Sorry, sir, I can explain. You see, I had a date and it ran a little late. I ran to catch the bus but I missed it. So I hailed a cab but it broke down. I managed to find a farm and bought a horse but it dropped dead. In the end I had to run ten miles, and now I'm here!'

The sergeant was highly sceptical about this explanation, but at least the soldier had made it back eventually, so he let him off this time. A couple of minutes later, eight more of his men ran up to the sergeant, panting. He asked them why they were late. Each told the same story.

'Sorry, sir. I had a date and it ran a little late. I ran to catch the bus but I missed it. So I hailed a cab but it broke down. I managed to find a farm and bought a horse but it dropped dead. In the end I had to run ten miles, and now I'm here!'

The sergeant eyed them suspiciously but since he had let the first man go, he decided that it was only fair to excuse them, too. A few minutes later, the tenth and last soldier ran up to him, panting heavily.

'Sorry, sir. I had a date and it ran a little late. I ran to catch the bus but I missed it. So I hailed a cab but . . .'

'Let me guess,' interrupted the sergeant. 'It broke down.'

'No, sir. There were so many dead horses in the road, it took forever to get round them.'

Through the night sky, a navy captain was able to make out a light dead ahead on collision course with his ship. He immediately sent a signal: 'Change your course ten degrees east.'

The mystery light signalled back: 'Change yours

ten degrees west.'

Angered by this, the captain sent another signal: 'I'm a navy captain. Change your course, sir!'

The signal came back: 'I'm a seaman, second class. Change your course, sir!'

Furious at such insubordination, the captain sent another signal: 'I'm a battleship – I'm not changing course.'

The reply came back: 'And I'm a lighthouse.'

A royal castle was under siege from an infidel army. The only hope was to send one of the knights to get help, but the problem was that all of the horses had been killed in the battle.

'Somehow we must get help,' said the king.

'I know, sire,' said the leader of his army, 'but we have no horses. If a knight sets off on foot, he will be slain at once.'

'Is there not another animal he can ride?' suggested the king. 'What about that mighty wolfhound? It could surely bear the weight of a man.'

'No, no,' pleaded the army leader. 'The wolfhound is too dangerous. Look at its snarling teeth. I wouldn't send a knight out on a dog like this.'

A naval admiral and an Army general were fishing together on a lake when a storm blew up and capsized their boat. Both men were left floundering helplessly in the water. Eventually the general managed to right the boat and clamber into it. He then rescued the admiral from drowning by getting him to hang onto an oar.

As the admiral was dragged into the boat, he puffed: 'Please don't say a word to anyone about this. If the Navy knew I couldn't swim, I'd be disgraced.'

'Don't worry,' said the general. 'Your secret is safe with me. I'd hate my men to find out that I couldn't walk on water.'

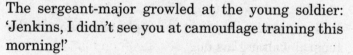

The sergeant-major growled at the young soldier: 'Jenkins, I didn't see you at camouflage training this morning!'

The soldier replied: 'Thank you very much, sir.'

An old sea captain was quizzing a young naval student. The captain said: 'What steps would you take if you were out at sea and a sudden storm came up on the starboard?'

'I'd throw out an anchor, sir,' replied the student.

'What would you do if another storm sprang up aft?'

'I'd throw out another anchor, sir.'

'But what if a third storm sprang up forward?'

'I'd throw out another anchor, captain.'

'Just a minute, son. Where in the world are you getting all these anchors?'

'From the same place you're getting all your storms, sir.'

Why didn't the sailors play cards?

– Because the captain was sitting on the deck.

An army private was out one night when he met the general walking his dog.

'Nice night, soldier,' said the general.

'Uh, yes, sir,' replied the private nervously.

Pointing to his dog, the general said: 'This is a golden retriever – the best breed of dog to train.'

'Uh, yes, sir,' agreed the private.

'I got this dog for my wife,' said the general.

The private said: 'Good trade, sir.'

A cargo plane was preparing for departure from a US Air Force base in Greenland, and the crew were waiting for the truck to arrive so that the aircraft's sewage tank could be pumped out. The aircraft commander was growing impatient. Not only did the truck show up late but the airman carrying out the task was extremely slow at pumping out the tank. Finally the commander snapped and vowed to punish the airman for being so slow.

The airman replied: 'Sir, I have no stripes, it is twenty degrees below zero, I'm stationed in Greenland miles from civilization, and I'm pumping sewage out of airplanes. Just what are you going to do to punish me?'

Why are soldier so tired on 1 April?
– Because they've just had a thirty-one-day March.

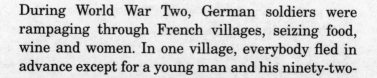

During World War Two, German soldiers were rampaging through French villages, seizing food, wine and women. In one village, everybody fled in advance except for a young man and his ninety-two-

41

year-old grandmother who refused to be driven out by the Germans. When the German tanks rumbled into the near-deserted village, the soldiers cornered the young man.

'Bring us food!' they ordered.

'All I have left is a loaf of bread,' he replied meekly.

'War is war,' said the soldiers, and they forced him to hand over the last crumbs of bread.

Then they yelled: 'Bring us wine!'

'All I have left is less than half a bottle,' said the young man.

'War is war,' insisted the soldiers, and they made him hand over the remainder of the bottle of wine.

Then the soldiers shouted: 'Bring us a woman!'

'But there is only one woman left in the village,' protested the young man.

'War is war,' barked the soldiers.

So the young man fetched his ninety-two-year-old grandmother. The German soldiers took one look at her and said: 'Uh, perhaps we will let you off this time.'

'No way,' said Grandma. 'War is war.'

Art and Books

In an art gallery, a woman was studying two near-identical pictures by the same artist. Both showed a glass of champagne, a basket of bread rolls, a bowl of salad, and a plate of smoked salmon. Yet one painting was priced at a hundred dollars, the other at a hundred and twenty-five dollars. So she asked the gallery owner to explain why one was more expensive than the other.

'It's obvious,' said the gallery owner, indicating the more expensive painting. 'You get two extra slices of smoked salmon in that one.'

An artist and his model were involved in a passionate embrace on his studio couch when he suddenly heard a key turning in the door.

'Quick!' he said. 'It's my wife. Take your clothes off and pretend we're working!'

A man walked into a bookshop and said: 'I'd like to buy a book by Shakespeare.'

'Yes, sir,' replied the sales assistant. 'Which one?'

'William, of course,' said the man.

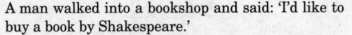

On a visit to an art gallery, a man was puzzled by what appeared to be a blank canvas. So when he spotted the artist, he asked him what it was supposed to be.

'That, sir, is a cow grazing,' said the artist with pride.

'Where's the grass?' asked the visitor.

'The cow's eaten it, sir.'

'Well, where's the cow?'

The artist turned to him and said: 'Surely you don't think the cow would be foolish to stay after she had eaten all the grass?'

A man went into a bookshop and asked the sales assistant: 'Where's the self-help section?'

She said: 'If I told you, it would defeat the purpose.'

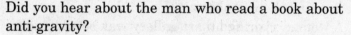

Did you hear about the man who read a book about anti-gravity?
– It was impossible to put down.

While working at home, Pablo Picasso surprised a burglar. The intruder escaped, but Picasso told police he could draw a picture of the suspect. On the basis of his drawing, police arrested a three-eyed woman, Adolf Hitler, a washing machine and the Eiffel Tower.

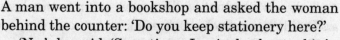

A man went into a bookshop and asked the woman behind the counter: 'Do you keep stationery here?'

'No,' she said. 'Sometimes I wriggle about a bit.'

A man went into a library and asked where he could find books on suicide.

'Second shelf on the right,' replied the librarian.

'But I've already looked in that section,' said the man, 'and it's empty.'

'I'm not surprised,' said the librarian. 'They don't often bring them back.'

A woman visiting an art gallery was bewildered by some of the paintings being exhibited. One picture was purple with vivid yellow swirls and the one next to it was bright red with lime green blobs. Since the artist was standing nearby, she took the opportunity to remonstrate with him.

'I'm sorry,' she said, 'but I simply don't understand your paintings.'

He replied haughtily: 'I paint what I feel inside me.'

'Oh,' she said. 'Have you tried Alka-Seltzer?'

A chicken walked into a library, went up to the desk and said: 'Book, book, book, book.'

The librarian handed the chicken a book and the bird left.

Ten minutes later, the chicken returned, tossed the book on the desk and said: 'Book, book, book, book.'

The librarian handed the chicken a different book and the chicken left.

Ten minutes later, the chicken brought the book back, threw it on the desk and said: 'Book, book, book, book.'

The librarian handed the chicken a third book but this time decided to follow the bird. He saw the chicken hurry off down the street and stop at the village pond where a frog was sitting on a lily pad. The chicken showed the book to the frog but the frog shook its head and said: 'Read-it, read-it, read-it.'

An artist asked the gallery owner if there had been any interest in his paintings that were currently on display.

'I have good news and bad news,' replied the gallery owner. 'The good news is that a gentleman enquired about your work and wondered whether it would appreciate in value after your death. When I told him it would, he bought all twenty of your paintings.'

'That's wonderful!' exclaimed the artist. 'So what's the bad news?'

'The man was your doctor.'

Bankers

A new schoolteacher was getting to know the children by asking them their name and what their father did for a living.

The first little girl said: 'My name is Kelly and my Daddy is a builder.'

The second child said: 'My name is Kylie and my Daddy works in a factory.'

And so it went on until one little boy said: 'My name is David and my Dad is a stripper in a gay bar.'

The teacher gasped in horror and quickly changed the subject. Later in the school yard the teacher approached David privately and asked if it was really true that his father danced naked in a gay bar.

David blushed and said: 'No, he's really a banker,

but I'm just too embarrassed to tell anyone.'

Two tigers were walking in single file through the jungle. Suddenly the tiger at the back began licking the butt of the tiger in front.

'Cut it out,' said the first tiger.

The second tiger apologized and they continued walking.

Five minutes later, the second tiger again started licking the butt of the first tiger.

'Will you stop doing that?' snarled the first tiger.

The second tiger apologized, and they continued on their way.

Five minutes later, the second tiger again licked the first tiger's butt.

'What is it with you?' hissed the first tiger, turning angrily and baring his claws.

'I'm really sorry,' said the second tiger. 'I didn't mean to upset you. But earlier today I ate a banker and I'm trying to get the taste out of my mouth.'

What's the difference between a banker and a vampire?
– A vampire sucks blood at night.

What's the difference between a banker and a trampoline?
– You take off your boots to jump on a trampoline.

A city banker was driving along in his stretch limo when he saw a humble man eating grass by the roadside. The banker ordered his chauffeur to stop, wound down the car window and called over to the man: 'Why are you eating grass?'

'Because, sir,' he replied, 'we don't have enough money for proper food.'

'Come with me then,' said the banker.

'But sir, I have a wife and six children.'

'That's okay,' said the banker. 'Bring them all along.'

The man and his family climbed gratefully into the banker's limo. 'Sir, you are too kind. How can I ever thank you for taking all of us with you, offering a new home to total strangers?'

'No, you don't understand,' said the banker. 'The grass at my mansion is four feet high. No lawn mower will cut it!'

What's the difference between an investment banker and someone who lost all his money betting on horses?
– A tie.

A young man went to see a bank manager with a view to extending his overdraft. At first, the manager refused even to consider the request but when the young man pleaded with him, he reconsidered.

'I'll tell you what I'll do,' said the bank manager. 'I'm a sporting man and I enjoy a wager. I've got a glass eye and if you can tell which one it is, I'll extend your overdraft.'

'It's your left eye,' said the young man without hesitation.

'That's correct,' said the bank manager. 'How did you know?'

The young man replied: 'Because it's a damn sight more sympathetic than your right eye.'

What does a banker use for birth control?
– His personality.

What's the difference between a no-claims bonus and a banker's bonus?
– You lose your no-claims bonus after a crash.

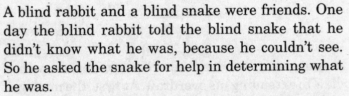

A blind rabbit and a blind snake were friends. One day the blind rabbit told the blind snake that he didn't know what he was, because he couldn't see. So he asked the snake for help in determining what he was.

The blind snake slithered up to the blind rabbit, felt it all over and said: 'You have long, furry ears and a short little tail. You must be a rabbit.'

The blind rabbit was delighted with the news, and agreed to repay the favour so that the blind snake could find out what he was.

The blind rabbit felt the blind snake all over and finally declared: 'You're cold, you're slimy and you don't have any balls. You must be a banker.'

What do you say to a hedge fund manager who can't sell anything?
– 'Quarter pounder with fries, please.'

Bars

A snake slithered into a bar and asked the bartender for a beer. 'Sorry,' said the bartender, 'I'm afraid I can't serve you.'

'Why not?' asked the snake.

'Because you can't hold your drink.'

A neutron walked into a bar and said to the bartender: 'How much for a beer?'

The bartender said: 'For you, no charge.'

A man walked into a bar and said: 'Bartender, give me two shots – one for me and one for my buddy here.'

The bartender asked: 'Do you want both drinks now or do you want me to wait till your buddy arrives to pour his?'

'No, it's okay,' said the man. 'I've got my best buddy in my pocket here.' And with that, he pulled out a little three-inch-high man from his pocket.

'That's amazing,' said the bartender. 'Can he walk?'

The man flicked a coin down to the end of the bar and said to his tiny friend: 'Hey, Kev, go and get that coin.'

Kev duly ran along the bar, fetched the coin and brought it back to the man.

The bartender was impressed. 'What else can he do?' he asked. 'Can he dance?'

'Sure he can dance,' said the man. 'Come on, Kev, show the bartender your favourite jig.'

And with that the little fellow did a dance on the bar.

'Hey, he's great!' laughed the bartender. 'Tell me, can he talk, too?'

'Talk?' said the man. 'Sure he talks. Hey, Kev, tell him about that time we were on safari in Africa and you insulted that witch doctor.'

A woman walked into a bar with a newt perched on her shoulder. She ordered a drink for herself and one for the newt.

'What's its name?' asked the bartender.

'Tiny,' said the woman.

'Why do you call it Tiny?'

'Because he's my newt.'

David Hasselhoff walked into a bar and ordered a beer.

The bartender said: 'It's a pleasure to serve you, Mr Hasselhoff.'

'Just call me Hoff,' said the actor.

'Sure,' said the bartender. 'No hassle.'

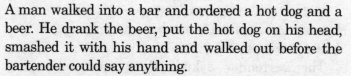

A man walked into a bar and ordered a hot dog and a beer. He drank the beer, put the hot dog on his head, smashed it with his hand and walked out before the bartender could say anything.

The man returned the next day and once again he ordered a hot dog and a beer. The bartender watched in amazement as the man drank the beer, put the hot dog on his head, smashed it with his hand and walked out.

The man was back again the following day and placed his usual order of a hot dog and a beer. But this time the bartender decided to catch him out, saying: 'I'm sorry, sir. We're out of hot dogs.'

'Very well,' said the man. 'I'll have a cheeseburger and a beer.'

He drank the beer, put the cheeseburger on his head, smashed it with his hand and headed for the door.

'Wait!' shouted the bartender, unable to contain his curiosity any longer. 'Why did you smash that cheeseburger on your head?'

The man replied: 'Because you didn't have any hot dogs.'

Two fonts walked into a bar. The bartender said: 'Sorry, we don't want your type in here.'

A mushroom walked into a bar and announced: 'The drinks are on me!'

The bartender asked: 'Why are you buying everybody drinks?'

The mushroom replied: 'Because I'm a fungi.'

The bartender asked a man sitting at the bar: 'What'll you have?'

The man answered: 'A scotch, please.'

The bartender handed him the drink and said: 'That'll be five dollars.'

The man said: 'What do you mean? I don't owe you anything for this.'

A lawyer sitting nearby overheard the conversation. He said to the bartender: 'The customer's got a point. In the original offer, which constitutes a binding contract upon acceptance, there was no stipulation of remuneration.'

The bartender was predictably unhappy, but said to the man: 'Okay, I'll let you off this time, but don't ever let me catch you in here again.'

The next day, the same man walked into the bar. The bartender said: 'What the hell are you doing in here? I thought I told you to keep away from this place. I can't believe you've got the nerve to come back.'

The man said innocently: 'What are you talking about? I've never been in this bar in my life.'

Fearing that he had made a mistake, the bartender backed down. 'I'm very sorry,' he said, 'but the likeness is uncanny. You must have a double.'

'That's very kind of you,' said the man. 'I'll have a scotch.'

A grasshopper walked into a bar. The bartender said: 'Hey, we have a drink named after you.'

The grasshopper looked at him and said: 'You have a drink named Derek?'

A piece of black tarmac walked into a bar and said to the bartender: 'Give me a pint and make it quick because I'm tough and I'm scared of nobody.'

Just then a piece of red tarmac walked into the bar, whereupon the black tarmac immediately fled to the toilet.

Ten minutes later, the black tarmac re-emerged and asked the bartender nervously: 'Has he gone yet?'

The bartender laughed: 'I thought you said you were scared of nobody! So what's the big deal with the red tarmac?'

The black tarmac said: 'Trust me, nobody messes with him. He's a cycle path.'

A piece of string walked into a bar, hopped onto a stool and shouted to the bartender: 'Gimme a drink!'

The bartender angrily picked up the piece of string and threw it out into the street.

The piece of string thought: 'I'll show him. I'll go back in disguise. He won't know it's me and at the last minute I'll humiliate him.' So the string contorted its body into a different shape and frizzed its hair in an afro. Then it went back into the bar, hopped onto a stool and yelled: 'Gimme a drink!'

The bartender said: 'You're that piece of string I threw out a few minutes ago.'

The piece of string said: 'I'm a frayed knot.'

A cowboy walked into a saloon wearing a coconut-filled chocolate bar in place of a hat.

'What's up with him?' the bartender asked one of the regulars.

'Oh, he's got a bounty on his head.'

A young girl walked into a bar and asked for a double vodka.

The barman looked at her suspiciously and asked: 'How old are you?'

'Fifteen,' answered the girl brazenly.

'Fifteen?!' yelled the barman. 'Are you trying to get me into trouble?'

'Maybe later,' said the girl, 'but for now I'll just have the vodka.'

A sausage walked into a bar and asked for a drink. The bartender said: 'Sorry, we don't serve food.'

A man walked into a smart city centre bar and sat down on a stool. The bartender said: 'What can I get you to drink, sir? How about a nice relaxing beer? We've got a special brew on offer this evening.'

'I'm sorry,' replied the man loftily, 'I don't drink alcohol. I tried it once but I didn't like it and I haven't touched a drop since.'

Being a friendly sort, the bartender thought he would try and strike up conversation by offering the man a cigar. 'You can't smoke it in here, of course,' he said, 'but you could keep it for later.'

'No thank you,' said the man with a sneer. 'I don't smoke. I tried it once but I didn't like it and I haven't smoked since. Listen, I appreciate you are merely trying to be sociable but the fact is that I wouldn't be in this place at all but for the fact that I'm waiting for my son.'

To which the bartender remarked: 'Your only child, I presume?'

60

A woman walked into a bar and asked for a double entendre. So the bartender gave her one.

Charles Dickens walked into a bar. The bartender said: 'Olive or twist?'

A man walked into a bar and ordered a glass of white wine. After taking a sip of the wine, he hurled the rest of the glass into the bartender's face. Before the bartender could recover from the shock, the man started weeping.

'I'm really sorry,' he sobbed. 'I keep doing that to bartenders. I can't tell you how embarrassing it is to have a compulsion like this.'

Far from being angry, the bartender was sympathetic and suggested that the man see an analyst about his problem. 'I happen to have the name of a good psychiatrist,' said the bartender. 'My brother and my wife both go to him, and they say he's the best there is.'

Three months later, the man returned to the same bar. The bartender remembered him straight away. 'Did you do what I suggested?' he asked, pouring the man a glass of white wine.

'I certainly did,' said the man. 'I've been seeing that psychiatrist you recommended for two sessions every week.' Then he took a sip of the wine and threw the rest of the glass into the bartender's face.

The flustered bartender wiped his face with a towel. 'The doctor doesn't seem to be doing you any good,' he spluttered.

'On the contrary,' insisted the man. 'He's done me the world of good.'

'But you threw the wine in my face again!'

'Yes, but it doesn't embarrass me anymore.'

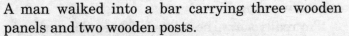

A man walked into a bar carrying three wooden panels and two wooden posts.

'You can't bring those in here,' said the bartender.

'Why not?' asked the man.

'They may cause a fence.'

Jesus walked into a bar and asked for a glass of water, which he promptly turned into wine.

'What do you think you're doing?' yelled the bartender.

Jesus replied: 'Well, I'm not paying your prices for a glass of Sauvignon Blanc.'

Two hydrogen atoms walked into a bar. One said: 'Oh dear, I think I've lost an electron.'

The other said: 'Are you sure?'

The first said: 'Yes, I'm positive.'

A bartender was just locking up for the night when there was a knock on the door. He opened the door to find a snail sitting there.

'What do you want?' asked the bartender.

'I want a drink,' said the snail.

'Go away,' said the bartender. 'We're closed.'

'Please,' begged the snail, 'I'm desperate for a drink.'

'I'm sorry,' repeated the bartender. 'We're closed.'

'Just one drink,' pleaded the snail.

'No,' snapped the bartender – and with that he kicked the snail down the street and slammed the door.

Eight months later, the bartender was again locking up when he heard a knock on the door. He opened the door to see the same snail sitting there.

The snail said: 'What did you do that for?'

A man walked into a bar but the bartender said: 'Sorry, I can't serve you unless you're wearing a tie.'

The man said: 'Okay, I'll be right back.'

He went to his car to search for something suitable but all he could find was a set of jump cables. So he tied them around his neck, went back into the bar and asked: 'Is this okay?'

The bartender said: 'Well, alright, but don't start anything.'

Battle of the Sexes

Three men were walking in the country when they came to a wide, raging river. They needed to get to the other side, but had no idea how to do so.

The first man prayed to God: 'Please, God, give me the strength to cross this river.' And POOF! God gave him powerful arms and strong legs, and he was able to swim across the mighty river in two hours.

Seeing this, the second man prayed: 'Please, God, give me the strength and ability to cross this river.' And POOF! God gave him a rowing boat, and he was able to row across the river in an hour.

The third man saw how this tactic worked for the other two, and so he prayed: 'Please, God, give me the strength, ability and intelligence to cross this river.' And POOF! God turned him into a woman.

She looked at a map, and then walked across the bridge.

What's a man's idea of a romantic night out?
– A candlelit football stadium.

What do a toilet and an anniversary have in common?
– Men always miss them.

Why don't men eat between meals?
– There is no 'between' meals.

A little girl asked her mother: 'How did the human race appear?'

The mother answered: 'God made Adam and Eve, they had children and that's how all mankind was made.'

Two days later, the girl asked her father the same question.

The father answered: 'Many years ago there were monkeys from which the human race evolved.'

The confused girl returned to her mother and said:

'Mum, how is it possible that you told me the human race was created by God and Dad said it developed from monkeys?'

'Well, darling,' said the mother, 'it's very simple. I told you about my side of the family and your father told you about his.'

What do you call an intelligent, handsome, sensitive man?
– A rumour.

What should you give a man who has everything?
– A woman to show him how to work it.

Why do men find it difficult to make eye contact?
– Because breasts don't have eyes.

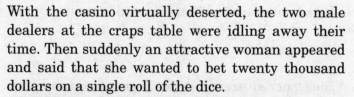

With the casino virtually deserted, the two male dealers at the craps table were idling away their time. Then suddenly an attractive woman appeared and said that she wanted to bet twenty thousand dollars on a single roll of the dice.

'Certainly, madam,' they said, happy to relieve the boredom.

'There's just one thing though,' she added. 'I hope you don't mind, but playing topless always brings me luck. So as there's hardly anyone about, would you mind if I took my top and bra off?'

So she removed her top and her bra, threw the dice and yelled: 'I've won! I've won! I can't believe it!' Then she scooped up the money, picked up her clothes and left.

The two dealers were stunned. 'What did she roll anyway?' asked one.

'I don't know,' said the other. 'I thought you were watching the dice!'

Why do men marry virgins?
– Because they can't stand criticism.

How does a man show he's planning for the future?
– He buys two cases of beer instead of one.

A man parked his car at the supermarket and was walking past an empty trolley when he heard a woman ask: 'Excuse me, do you want that trolley?'

'No, he answered, 'I'm only after one thing.'
'Huh,' she mumbled. 'Typical man!'

Why are men like cycling helmets?
– Because they're useful in an emergency but the rest of the time they just look silly.

What do train sets and breasts have in common?
– They're intended for children, but it's usually the men who end up playing with them.

A man turned to his wife and said sarcastically: 'I don't know why you wear a bra – you've got nothing to put in it.'

She replied: 'Well, you wear underpants, don't you?'

What a woman says

'This place is a mess!

Come on, you and I need to clean.

Your stuff is on the floor

And you'll have no clothes to wear

If we don't do the laundry right now.'

And what a man hears

'Blah, blah, blah, blah, COME ON,

Blah, blah, blah, blah, YOU AND I

Blah, blah, blah, blah, ON THE FLOOR

Blah, blah, blah, blah, NO CLOTHES

Blah, blah, blah, blah, RIGHT NOW.'

Things That Men Can't Do

Replace an empty roll of toilet paper.

Make a bed.

Find a matching pair of socks.

Watch TV without constantly checking what's on the other channels.

Hand over custody of the TV remote.

Go to the supermarket without buying junk food.

Throw out old clothes that no longer fit them.

Fold clean clothes.

Clean a bathroom.

Throw away an empty milk carton.

Refrain from scratching their crotch in public.

Hang up wet towels.

Read instructions.

Suffer a common cold without thinking they're going to die.

Go to the pub for just one drink.

Wrap a gift.

Sit still through an entire movie.

Try to fix something without hitting it first.

Things That Women Can't Do

Know anything about a car except its colour.

Understand the offside rule in soccer.

Go more than two minutes without sending a text message.

Understand a movie plot.

Read a map.

Lift.

Throw.

Catch.

Park.

Fart.

Play pool.

Pee out of a train window.

Argue without shouting.

Get told off without crying.

Understand fruit machines.

Clear their throat noisily.

Eat a kebab whilst walking.

Walk past a shoe shop.

Not comment on a stranger's clothes.

Use small amounts of toilet paper.

Drink a pint gracefully.

Get a round in.

Throw a punch.

Take less than half an hour in the bathroom.

Set a DVD recorder.

Buy a purse that fits into their pocket.

Get to the point.

How do men exercise on the beach?
– By sucking their stomach in every time they see a bikini.

What's a man's idea of helping with the housework?
– Lifting his legs so you can vacuum.

What's the difference between a G-spot and a golf ball?
– Men will actually search for a golf ball.

What does it mean when a man is in your bed gasping for breath and calling your name?
– You didn't hold the pillow down long enough.

A man said to his drinking buddy: 'My wife is the double of Kate Moss.'

'Really?'

'Yes. Kate Moss weighs eight stone and my wife weighs sixteen stone.'

How many men does it take to open a beer?
– None. It should be opened by the time she brings it to you.

What's long and hard and makes women moan?
– An ironing board.

If a motorcyclist runs into a woman, who's to blame?
– The motorcyclist: he shouldn't have been riding in the kitchen.

'Good afternoon, ladies,' said Sherlock Holmes to three women sitting on a bench in a London park.

'Do you know those women?' asked his faithful companion, Dr Watson.

'No,' said Holmes as the pair continued walking. 'I don't know the spinster, the prostitute and the new bride.'

'Good heavens, Holmes!' exclaimed Watson. 'If you don't know them, how can you be so sure that they are what you say?'

'Elementary, my dear Watson,' explained Holmes, glancing back. 'Observe how they are eating their bananas.'

'So?'

'Well, Watson, the spinster holds the banana in her left hand and uses her right hand to break the banana into small pieces which she then puts in her mouth.'

'I see what you mean, Holmes. That's amazing! What about the prostitute?'

'She holds the banana in both hands and crams it into her mouth.'

'Holmes, you've surpassed yourself! But how do you know that the other woman is a new bride?'

'Simple,' replied Holmes. 'She holds the banana in

her left hand and uses her right hand to push her
head towards the banana.'

What should you give a woman who has
everything?
– Penicillin.

If Women Ruled the World . . .

Men would get 'reputations' for sleeping around.

PMS would be a legitimate defence in court.

Singles bars would have metal detectors to weed out
men hiding wedding rings in their pockets.

A man would no longer be considered a 'good catch'
simply because he has a pulse.

All toilet seats would be nailed down.

Men would pay as much attention to their woman as
to their car.

Overweight men would be encouraged to wear girdles.

Men who design women's shoes would be forced to wear them.

During a midlife crisis, men would get hot flushes and women would date nineteen-year-olds.

Eating chocolate would be compulsory.

Men would not be allowed to eat gas-producing foods within two hours of bedtime.

Men would be judged entirely by their looks, women by their accomplishments.

There would be a cure for stretch marks.

Shopping would be considered an aerobic activity.

Men would HAVE to get *Playboy* for the articles because there'd be no pictures.

Maternity leave would last for three years – with full pay.

What food reduces a woman's sex drive by ninety per cent?
– Wedding cake.

Why do women have smaller feet than men?
– So they can stand closer to the kitchen sink.

How can a man tell if his wife is dead?
– The sex is the same but the dishes pile up.

What do you call a woman with one leg?
– Eileen.

What do you call a woman who sets fire to her credit card bill?
– Bernadette.

What do you call a woman with excessive hair on her top lip?
– Tash.

What's the difference between a woman and a mobile phone?
– You can put a mobile phone on silent.

Why is an ex-wife like an inflamed appendix?
– She causes a lot of pain and suffering and after she's removed you realize you didn't need her anyway.

What would have happened if the birth of Jesus had been attended by Three Wise Women instead of Three Wise Men? They would have asked for directions, arrived on time, helped deliver the baby, cleaned the stable, made a casserole, and brought practical gifts. But what would they have said as they left?

'Did you see the sandals Mary was wearing with that gown?'

'That baby doesn't look anything like Joseph!'

'Virgin?! Who's she kidding? I knew her in school!'

'Can you believe they allowed all those disgusting animals in there?'

'I heard that Joseph isn't even working at the moment!'

'I wouldn't bet on getting your casserole dish back in a hurry!'

Birds

A vicar new to the area visited a little old lady who owned a pet parrot. He noticed that the bird had a ribbon tied to each leg.

'What are the ribbons for?' he enquired.

The old lady said: 'If I pull the left ribbon, he sings "Clementine", and if I pull the right ribbon, he sings "Yankee Doodle Dandy".'

'And what happens if you pull both ribbons at the same time?' asked the vicar.

'I fall off the bloody perch!' said the parrot.

A man started bidding for a parrot at auction. He thought the bird would cost around sixty dollars, but a mystery bidder kept stepping in at the last minute to push up the price. Soon the price had risen to over a hundred and twenty dollars, more than double what the man had intended to pay. By now he was more determined than ever to buy the bird but decided to set an absolute limit of two hundred dollars. If he couldn't get the parrot for that price, he would withdraw from the bidding.

Prompted by the mystery bidder, the price continued to soar and the man put in his final bid of two hundred dollars.

The auctioneer said: 'Going once . . .'

The man waited with baited breath.

'Going twice . . .'

No sound from the mystery bidder.

'Sold!' The man breathed a big sigh of relief.

As he was paying for the bird, he said to the auctioneer: 'I hope this parrot can talk. I'll be cross if I've paid that much money for him only to find he can't talk.'

'Of course he can talk,' said the auctioneer. 'Who do you think was bidding against you?'

A penguin walked into a bar and asked the barman: 'Have you seen my brother?'

'I don't know,' said the barman. 'What does he look like?'

One day, a young sooty tern was flying out over the sea with its parents when the mummy bird ran into a cliff and dropped to the ground. Oblivious to his mate's fate, the father tern flew on, but the youngster swooped to the foot of the cliff in a bid to save her. Alas, the mummy tern was already dead, and the tearful youngster was taken under the wing of a family of seagulls.

A week later, the head of the seagull family announced: 'You are an extremely well-behaved bird, but I'm afraid we can't keep you. Instead we're going to try and find a tern who can adopt you, to act as a replacement mummy.'

So the seagull put an ad in the local paper: One good tern deserves a mother.

A circus owner walked into a bar and saw everyone gathered around a table. On the table was a duck tap-dancing on an upturned flower pot. The circus owner was so impressed that he bought the duck and the flower pot for a thousand dollars.

People came from miles around to see the duck's heavily promoted debut in the Big Top but to widespread disappointment, the duck didn't dance a step. The next day, the angry circus owner returned to the bar to seek out the man who had sold the duck to him.

'That duck is a fraud,' raged the circus owner. 'He hasn't danced a step for me.'

'That's odd. Did you remember to light the candle under the flower pot?'

Why do birds fly south in the water?
– Because it's too far to walk.

A man bought a budgie from a pet shop but was disappointed when it refused to talk. So he went back to the shop to complain.

'I've had this budgie for three months,' said the man, 'and he hasn't uttered a single word. What should I do?'

'Try getting him a mirror,' suggested the shop owner. 'Budgies love to look at their own reflection. You'll see, soon you won't be able to stop him talking.'

So the man bought a mirror, but still the budgie

wouldn't talk. Two weeks later, the man returned to the shop.

'Try buying him a ladder,' advised the shop owner. 'They love climbing. He won't stop talking once he's got a ladder.'

So the man bought a ladder, but the budgie remained silent. Two weeks later, the man was back at the pet shop.

'Try getting him a bell,' said the shop owner. 'I'm sure that will work. The sound of music will encourage him to talk.'

So the man bought a bell. Two weeks later, he returned to the pet shop.

'Finally my budgie said something!' he announced. 'He looked in his mirror, climbed up his ladder, rang his bell, said a few words, and then dropped dead off his perch.'

'Oh dear!' said the shop owner. 'What did he say?'

'He said: "Doesn't that shop sell any bloody bird seed?"'

Two ducks were on honeymoon in a smart hotel. Just as they were about to make love, the male duck said: 'Oh no, I forget to bring any condoms! I'll ring down to room service.'

So he phoned room service and the woman there

said: 'Condoms? Certainly, sir. Would you like them on your bill?'

'No,' said the duck. 'I'd suffocate.'

Why does a flamingo lift up one leg?
– Because if it lifted up both it would fall over.

What happens to ducks before they grow up?
– They grow down.

A woman bought a parrot with beautiful plumage, but the only thing it could say was, 'Who is it?' After a few days she realized that the bird's colour clashed with the rest of the living room, so she called a decorator to give the room a new coat of paint. When he arrived to do the job, she had just gone to the Post Office to mail a letter, leaving the parrot in charge of the house.

The decorator knocked on the front door.

'Who is it?' squawked the parrot.

'It's the decorator.'

'Who is it?' repeated the parrot.

'It's the decorator.'

'Who is it?'

'It's the decorator!' yelled the man impatiently.

'Who is it?'

'It's the bloody decorator!'

'Who is it?'

'I said it's the decorator!'

And with that, the man suffered a fatal heart attack and collapsed on the doorstep.

A few minutes later, the woman returned home. Seeing the body on the step, she exclaimed: 'My God! Who is it?'

The parrot replied: 'It's the decorator!'

A burglar broke into a house and started to ransack the place in search of cash. As he passed the budgie's cage, the bird said: 'I can see you and so can Jesus.'

The burglar paid no attention and continued with his search. Again the budgie said: 'I can see you and so can Jesus.'

Irritated by the budgie's squawking, the burglar turned to the bird and growled: 'What are you going to do to stop me? You're only a budgie.'

'That's true,' replied the budgie, 'but Jesus is a Rottweiler.'

Why don't owls mate during a storm?
– Because it's too wet to woo.

A police officer saw a man driving a pickup truck full of penguins. He pulled the guy over and said: 'You can't drive around with penguins in this town. Take them to the zoo immediately.'

The next day, he saw the man still driving around with the penguins, and this time they were wearing sunglasses.

The cop said: 'I thought I told you to take these penguins to the zoo yesterday.'

'I did,' replied the man. 'And today I'm taking them to the beach.'

A chicken saw a duck standing by the side of the road. The chicken walked over to the duck and said: 'Don't do it, pal. You'll never hear the end of it!'

Birth

Two women sitting in the doctor's waiting room began discussing babies.

'I am desperate for a baby,' said one, 'but I fear it's never going to happen.'

'I used to think that,' said the other. 'But then everything changed. That's why I'm here. I'm going to have a baby in four months.'

'How did it all change?'

'I went to a faith healer.'

'But I've tried that. My husband and I went to one for nearly a year and it didn't help at all.'

The pregnant woman smiled and whispered: 'Next time, try going alone.'

A young man walked into a pharmacy to buy a packet of condoms. The sales clerk persuaded him to buy some multicoloured condoms, which were on special offer.

Nine months later, the young man returned to the drug store to buy a maternity bra.

'What bust?' asked the clerk.

'I think it was the red one,' said the young man.

A young couple were desperate to start a family but after nine years of trying they began to fear that they were destined never to have children. Having exhausted all medical advice, the wife read a magazine article about sperm donors and wondered whether they could be the way forward. She approached a few male friends to ask if they would be willing to donate their sperm but all declined on moral grounds. So, with her husband's full support, she contacted a stranger who was advertising his services as a sperm donor. He arranged to call on her at home the following Tuesday while her husband was at work. The wife was uneasy about the procedure anyway but couldn't bear the thought of going through with it while her husband was in the house.

On that same Tuesday a baby photographer

happened to be calling door-to-door in the neighbourhood. He called at the wife's house, and she answered the door, expecting the sperm donor.

'Good morning, madam,' said the photographer. 'You don't know me, but I've come to . . .'

'Yes, I know,' she interrupted. 'There's no need to explain. Come in. I've been expecting you.'

'Oh, really?' said the photographer, thinking that his advertising campaign must have paid off. 'I must say I do specialize in babies.'

'That's what my husband and I were hoping,' she said apprehensively. 'So tell me, where do we start?'

'Well, I usually try a couple on the bed, one on the couch and a couple outside in the garden. That always works for me.'

'I see,' she said. 'No wonder Peter and I haven't had much luck.'

'If we try several different positions and I shoot from five or six different angles, I'm sure you'll be satisfied with the results.'

'I do hope so,' she replied, becoming increasingly nervous. 'Can we get this over with quickly?'

'In my line of work I have to take my time,' he said. 'You can't rush these things. I'd love to be in and out in five minutes, but I think you'd be disappointed with that.'

'That's true,' she sighed knowingly.

The photographer opened his case and pulled out

a folder of baby pictures. 'This one was done on top of a bus,' he announced proudly.

'Really?' she said, a mixture of surprise and horror.

'And these twins turned out really well considering that their mother was difficult to work with.'

'In what way was she difficult?'

'She insisted that we go to the park. People were crowding four deep to watch, so it was really difficult to get the job done properly. It took over three and a half hours before we were finished. I was absolutely exhausted.'

By now the wife was sick with worry.

'Right,' he said. 'I'll just get my tripod.'

'Tripod?' she queried, ashen-faced.

'Yes, I need a tripod on which to rest my Canon.'

At that point the wife fainted.

Did you hear about the man whose wife asked him to go into town and buy a baby monitor?
– He couldn't find one anywhere, so he bought her an iguana instead.

A group of pregnant women and their partners were attending an antenatal class. The instructor was stressing the importance of keeping healthy during pregnancy.

'Exercise is good for you, ladies,' he said. Walking is particularly beneficial. And gentlemen, it wouldn't hurt you to take the time to go walking with your partner.'

Hearing this, one man called out: 'Is it okay if she carries a golf bag while we walk?'

Why don't the wives of bus drivers get pregnant?
– Because bus drivers have a habit of pulling out unexpectedly.

A young man was pacing up and down outside the maternity ward of a hospital. Meanwhile an older man was calmly reading a magazine. Suspecting that the older man was not a first-time father, the young man asked him: 'How long after the baby is born can you have sex with the mother?'

The older man looked up from his magazine and answered: 'It depends on whether she's in a public ward or a private ward.'

A woman was lying in hospital, giving birth. After twenty-five minutes of pushing, panting and sweating, the baby's head finally popped out. The baby took one look at the doctor and asked: 'Are you my daddy?'

'No, I'm not,' replied the startled doctor – and the baby popped back into the womb.

The obstetrician was immediately summoned to the ward. As soon as he arrived, the baby's head popped out again.

'Are you my daddy?' asked the baby.

'No, I'm not,' said the obstetrician.

The obstetrician decided to fetch the boy's father who had been waiting outside. 'The baby seems reluctant to come out,' said the medic. 'He keeps asking for his father, so would you come into the delivery room?'

The father entered the delivery room and the baby's head popped out again.

'Are you my daddy?' asked the baby.

The father knelt down and answered proudly: 'Yes, son, I'm your father.'

At this, the baby started tapping his index finger forcibly and repeatedly on the father's forehead and said: 'That's pretty damned annoying, isn't it?'

Children

A small boy came running out of the bathroom in tears.

'What's the matter, son?' asked his father.

'I dropped my toothbrush in the toilet,' said the boy.

'Never mind, son, but we'd better throw it out.'

So the father fished the toothbrush out of the toilet and put it in the garbage. When he returned, the boy was holding another toothbrush.

'Isn't that my toothbrush?' asked the father.

'Yes,' said the boy, 'and we'd better throw this one out, too, because it fell in the toilet last week.'

Little Johnny came into the house for dinner after playing with his little friend Sally. His parents asked him what he had been doing all afternoon.

He said: 'I played football for a while and then I proposed to Sally.'

His parents thought that was really sweet and, not wishing to make fun of him, went along with the idea. His father said: 'But, Johnny, you know being married is an expensive business. How are you going to manage?'

'Well,' said Johnny, 'with the seven dollars I get each week from you and the five dollars she gets from her mum and dad, we should be okay. I can always get a paper round.'

Suppressing a smile, his mother said: 'That's all very well, darling. But how will you and Sally manage if you have a baby?'

'Well,' said Johnny, 'so far – touch wood – we've been lucky.'

The head of an international company needed to speak urgently with one of his managers at the weekend, so he phoned him at home. The phone was answered by a small boy in a voice that was little more than a whisper.

'Hello,' said the boss. 'Is your daddy home?'

'Yes,' whispered the child.

'May I speak with him?'

'No.'

It was a word the boss wasn't accustomed to hearing. 'Well,' he continued, 'is your mummy there?'

'Yes,' whispered the boy.

'May I speak with her?'

'No.'

By now the boss was starting to lose patience. 'Listen, son,' he said, 'is anyone else there?'

'Yes,' said the boy, 'a policeman.'

The news took the boss by surprise. 'Well, may I speak with him?'

'No, he's busy,' whispered the boy.

'Busy doing what?'

'Talking to Daddy, Mummy and the firemen.'

Just then, the boss heard a strange whirring sound down the phone. 'What's that noise?' he asked.

'A helicopter,' whispered the boy.

'What exactly is going on here?' said the boss.

'The search team just landed the helicopter outside our house,' said the boy.

'What are they doing there?'

The boy whispered: 'They're looking for me.'

Little Johnny's dog Muffin was sick and the boy was worried that his dad would have bad news when he came back from seeing the vet. Sure enough, when his father returned home he said: 'I'm afraid it's not good news, son. The vet thinks Muffin's only got another few weeks to live.'

Hearing this, Johnny burst into tears.

Trying to console him, his father said: 'Muffin wouldn't want you to be sad. He'd want you to remember all the happy times you had together.'

Johnny rubbed his eyes. 'Can we give Muffin a funeral?'

'Of course we can,' said his father.

'Can I invite all my friends?'

'Sure you can.'

'And can we have cake and ice cream?'

'You can have whatever you want.'

'Dad,' said Johnny. 'Can we kill Muffin today?'

Two small boys were walking home from school. One said: 'I'm really worried. My dad works six days a week to give us a lovely home, plenty of food and great vacations. And my mum spends all day keeping the house clean, washing and ironing my clothes and cooking great meals, and then on three evenings she does a part-time job to earn us extra little luxuries.'

'Wow!' said his friend. 'You sound really lucky. So why are you worried?'

The first boy said: 'What if they try to escape?'

A boy was looking through the big, old family Bible when something fell out. It was a leaf from a tree that had been pressed between the pages.

'Mum, look what I found,' said the boy.

'What have you got there?' asked his mother as he showed her the leaf.

He said: 'I think it's Adam's suit!'

A young girl was looking at a picture book when she asked her mother: 'Mummy, where do babies come from?'

'The stork, darling,' replied the mother.

Satisfied with the answer, the girl returned to her book but a few moments later asked: 'Mummy, who keeps bad people from robbing our house?'

'The police, darling,' answered the mother.

The girl returned to her book, but seconds later she asked: 'Mummy, if our house was on fire, who would save us?'

'The fire department, darling,' said the mother.

The girl went back to her book but then asked: 'Mummy, if I'm sick, who will make me better?'

'The doctor, darling,' said the mother.

The girl looked at another picture in her book before asking: 'Mummy, where does our dinner come from?'

'The butcher, darling,' said the mother.

The girl then closed her book and asked: 'Mummy, what do we need Daddy for?'

The lifeguard at the swimming pool called over Little Johnny. 'You're not allowed to pee in the pool,' said the lifeguard. 'You're going to have to leave.'

'But everyone pees in the pool,' Johnny protested.

'Maybe,' said the lifeguard. 'But not from the diving board.'

A little boy wanted a new bicycle for Christmas. His mother said she didn't have enough money to buy him a new bike but suggested that if he wrote to Jesus promising to be a good boy in future, then maybe Jesus might be willing to get him one.

So the boy started writing a letter. 'Dear Jesus, I promise to be good for one year . . .' He then crossed that out and wrote: 'Dear Jesus, I promise to be good for one month.' Still he wasn't happy, so he crossed it out and wrote: 'Dear Jesus, I promise to be good for one week.' His head in a spin, he tore up the paper and went for a walk.

As he passed the local church, he noticed a nativity scene. When nobody was looking, he grabbed the figure of Mary, hid it under his coat and ran home.

There, he composed a new letter. 'Dear Jesus, if you ever want to see your mother again . . .'

A mother took her five-year-old son with her to the bank on a busy Friday. They got into line behind an overweight woman wearing a business suit, complete with pager. As the mother waited patiently, the boy looked at the woman in front and observed loudly: 'She's fat.'

The big woman turned around immediately and glared at the child, causing the embarrassed mother to reprimand him quietly.

However a minute later, the unrepentant boy

spread his hands as far as they would go and said loudly: 'I bet her butt is *that* wide!'

Again the woman turned and gave him a withering look, forcing the mother to give him a sterner telling off.

But a couple of minutes later the boy stated loudly: 'Look how the fat hangs over her belt!'

The woman turned and told the mother that she ought to teach her son some manners. The mother responded by issuing threats if he did not behave himself. The boy promised to keep quiet.

Moments later, the large woman reached the front of the queue but just as she did so, her pager began to emit its distinctive tone. The boy could not help himself. 'Run for your life, Mum!' he yelled in panic. 'She's backing up!'

An elderly man was walking down the street one day when he noticed a small boy struggling to press the doorbell at a house. However the boy was too short to reach. So the kindly old man walked up to the boy, placed a comforting hand on his shoulder and gave the doorbell a firm press.

'There,' said the old man, stepping back. 'Now what do we do, young man?'

The boy replied: 'We run like crazy!'

Two brothers aged seven and nine were always getting into trouble. Having tried everything to get them to behave, their parents decided as a last resort to contact a fire and brimstone preacher who had experienced some success in dealing with wayward children. The preacher agreed to help and asked to see the boys individually.

First he called in the seven-year-old, sat him down and asked sternly: 'Where is God?'

The boy didn't answer, so the preacher repeated the question, this time more forcefully. 'Where is God?'

Again the boy made no attempt to answer, so the cleric started shouting and waving his finger in the boy's face. 'Where is God?'

At that, the boy ran from the room and met up with his older brother outside.

'What happened?' asked the nine-year-old.

The younger boy replied: 'We're in big trouble this time. God is missing, and they think we did it!'

A young boy went into a grocery store and picked out a large box of laundry detergent. The grocer walked over and asked him if he had a lot of laundry to do.

'Oh no, I don't have any laundry to do,' said the boy. 'I'm going to wash my puppy.'

'You shouldn't use detergent on your puppy,' advised the grocer. 'It's very powerful. If you wash your dog in this, he'll get sick. In fact, it might even kill him.'

But the boy refused to listen and bought the detergent anyway.

A week later, he was back in the store buying some chocolate. The grocer asked him how his dog was.

'Oh, he died,' said the boy.

'I'm sorry to hear that,' said the grocer, 'but I did try to warn you about using that detergent on your puppy.'

'I don't think it was the detergent that killed him,' said the boy.

'Oh,' said the grocer. 'What was it then?'

'I think it was the spin cycle.'

When she got home from school, a six-year-old girl told her mother that Timmy Morrison had kissed her after class.

'How did that happen?' asked her mother, shocked by the revelation.

'It wasn't easy,' said the daughter. 'Three other girls had to hold him down for me!'

While his wife was enjoying a night out with her friends, a husband relaxed and watched TV. But he was interrupted when their ten-year-old son, who had been watching his own TV in his room, appeared in the doorway and asked: 'What's love juice?'

Choking on his beer, the dad decided that perhaps it was time to explain a few things to the boy. 'Well son,' he said, 'one day when you're older you'll meet a girl you really like and you'll get aroused and your penis will get hard. You will touch the girl all over and when you reach the top of her leg it will feel wet. This is her love juice coming out of her vagina, which means that she is ready for sexual intercourse.'

The son looked puzzled and said: 'Okay, Dad, thanks.'

As the boy was about to leave the room, the dad said: 'Hang on, son, what are you watching up there to make you ask such a question?'

The son replied: 'Wimbledon.'

Computers and the Internet

An artist, a lawyer and a computer programmer were discussing the merits of a mistress.

The artist enthused: 'A mistress has energy and passion and there is always that thrill of being discovered.'

But the lawyer warned: 'It can lead to a costly divorce and bankruptcy, so it's not worth the risk.'

The computer programmer said: 'Taking a mistress is the best thing that's ever happened to me. My wife thinks I'm with my mistress, my mistress thinks I'm at home with my wife, and I can spend all night on the computer!'

Preparing to move into a new house, Bill Gates phoned the building contractor.

Bill: 'There are a few issues we need to discuss.'

Contractor: 'You have your basic support option. Calls are free for the first thirty days but after that it's fifty dollars a call. Okay?'

Bill: 'Uh, yeah, I guess so. The first issue is the living room. It's a bit smaller than we anticipated.'

Contractor: 'Yes. Some compromises were made to have it out by the release date.'

Bill: 'We won't be able to fit all our furniture in there.'

Contractor: 'Well, you have two options. You can purchase a new, larger living room or you can use a stacker.'

Bill: 'What's a stacker?'

Contractor: 'It allows you fit twice as much furniture into a room, simply by stacking it. So you put your TV on the couch and your chairs on the table. The idea is you leave an empty spot so when you want to use some furniture you can unstack what you need and then put it back when you're finished with it.'

Bill: 'Uh, I'm not sure about that . . . Issue two is the light fittings. The bulbs we brought with us from our old home won't fit. The threads run the wrong way.'

Contractor: 'You'll have to upgrade to new bulbs.'

Bill: 'And the electrical outlets? The holes are round, not rectangular. How do I fix that?'

Contractor: 'Just uninstall and reinstall the electrical system.'

Bill: 'You're kidding!'

Contractor: 'No, it's the only way.'

Bill: 'Well, I have one last problem. Sometimes when I have guests over, someone will flush the toilet and it won't stop. The water pressure drops so low that the showers won't work.'

Contractor: 'That's a resource leakage problem. One fixture is failing to terminate and is hogging the resources, thereby preventing access from other fixtures.'

Bill: 'And how do I fix that?'

Contractor: 'Well, after each flush, you need to leave the house, turn off the water at the street, turn it back on, re-enter the house and then you can get back to work.'

Bill: 'This is crazy! What kind of product are you selling me?'

Contractor: 'If you don't like it, nobody made you buy it.'

Bill: 'When will it all be fixed?'

Contractor: 'In your next house, which we'll be ready to release sometime near the end of next year. Actually it was due out this year, but we've had some delays . . .'

Why Computers Are Male

In order to get their attention, you have to turn them on.

They have a lot of data but are still clueless.

They are supposed to help you solve problems, but half the time they are the problem.

As soon as you commit to one you realize that if you had waited a little longer you could have had a better model.

Big power surges knock them out for the night.

They'll usually do what you ask them to do, but they won't do more than they have to and they won't think of it on their own.

Why Computers Are Female

No one but their creator understands their internal logic.

They hear what you say, but not what you mean.

Even your smallest mistakes are immediately committed to memory for future reference.

You do the same thing for years, and suddenly it's wrong.

The native language they use to communicate with other computers is incomprehensible to everyone else.

As soon as you make a commitment to one, you find yourself spending half your monthly salary on accessories for it.

A computer programmer had not been seen for two weeks, so worried work colleagues notified the police. When officers broke down the door of his apartment, they found him dead in the shower, an empty bottle of shampoo lying next to his body.

The inquest stated that he had died from a combination of exposure and exhaustion, which left detectives baffled until they read the instructions on the shampoo bottle – 'Wet hair. Apply shampoo. Rinse. Repeat.'

A truck driver hauling a load of computers stopped at a roadside bar for a beer. As he entered, he saw a big sign on the door that read: 'COMPUTER NERDS NOT ALLOWED – ENTER AT YOUR OWN RISK.'

The bartender eyed the trucker suspiciously: 'I can smell computers on you. I hope you're not a nerd.'

'No, I'm not,' said the trucker, 'but I'm carrying a load of computers today. That's what the smell is.'

'That's okay then,' said the bartender, serving him his beer.

Just then, a skinny guy walked into the bar wearing black-rimmed glasses held together with tape and with a row of pens and pencils in his breast pocket. Without saying a word, the bartender pulled out a shotgun and shot him dead.

'What did you do that for?' asked the trucker.

'Don't worry,' said the bartender. 'The computer nerds are in season because they're overpopulating Silicon Valley. You don't even need a licence to shoot them.'

After finishing his drink, the trucker resumed his journey but half a mile down the highway he had to swerve violently to avoid another vehicle. The back doors of his truck fell open and his load of computers spilled out onto the road. By the time he had got round to the back of his truck to assess the damage, dozens of computer geeks had already gathered and were running off with the computers. He couldn't risk losing the entire load so, remembering the incident in the bar, he pulled out his gun and shot several of them dead on the spot.

Seconds later, a highway patrol car screeched to a halt and a police officer jumped out and ordered the trucker to stop shooting at once.

'What's wrong?' said the trucker. 'I thought computer nerds were in season.'

'They are,' said the officer. 'But you're not allowed to bait 'em!'

How can a woman stop her husband from reading her emails?
– Rename the file 'Instruction Manuals'.

At a software management engineering course, the participants were given an awkward question to answer: 'If you had just boarded an aeroplane and discovered that your team of programmers had been responsible for the flight control software, how many of you would disembark immediately?'

Everybody raised their hands except one man. When asked what he would do, he replied: 'I'd be quite happy to stay on board. Because with my team's software, the plane would be unlikely to even taxi as far as the runway, let alone take off!'

Signs That Your Cat Has Learned Your Internet Password

You start receiving emails from some guy called Fluffy.

There are traces of kitty litter in your keyboard.

eBay informs you that your five-hundred-dollar bid for a toy mouse has been successful.

Your hard drive contains a number of recently downloaded photos of roast chicken.

Your web browser has a new home page – http://www.catfancy.com

All dog websites have been deleted from 'My Favourite Places'.

Your mouse has teeth marks in it and a strange aroma of tuna.

Your history of recently visited sites shows several related to garden birds.

Three women were comparing their sex lives.

The first said: 'My husband is an architect. Our love-making has power, form and function.'

The second said: 'My husband is an artist. Our love-making has passion, emotion and vision.'

The third said: 'My husband works for Microsoft. When we make love he sits at the end of the bed in the dark telling me how great it will be when we finally get started.'

Crossing the Road Jokes

Why did the chicken cross the road? – He wanted to be poultry in motion.

Why did the chicken cross the road halfway? – Because she wanted to lay it on the line.

Why did the piece of chewing gum cross the road? – It was stuck to the chicken's foot.

Why did the rubber chicken cross the road? – To stretch his legs.

Why did the chicken cross the playground? – To get to the other slide.

Why did the chicken cross the basketball court? – He heard the referee calling fouls.

Why did the chicken cross the muddy road and not come back? – Because he didn't want to be a dirty double-crosser.

Why did the duck cross the road? – To prove he wasn't chicken.

Why did the giraffe cross the road? – It was the chicken's day off.

Why did the cow cross the road? – To get to the udder side.

Why did the turtle cross the road? – To get to the shell station.

Why did the sheep cross the road? – To get to the baa baa shop.

Why did the man with one arm cross the road? – To get to the second-hand shop.

Why did the hedgehog cross the road? – He wanted to see his flat mate.

Why didn't the skeleton cross the road? – Because it had no guts.

Why did the dinosaur cross the road? – Because chickens hadn't been invented yet.

Death

An archaeologist was digging in an Israeli desert when he came across a casket containing a mummy. After examining it, he called the curator of a museum to report: 'I've just discovered the three-thousand-year-old mummy of a man who died of heart failure.'

The curator said: 'Bring it in. We'll see if you're right.'

Six weeks later, the curator phoned the archaeologist. 'Congratulations! You were absolutely spot on about the mummy's age and cause of death. But how on earth did you know?'

'It was easy,' said the archaeologist. 'There was a piece of paper in his hand that said, "Ten thousand shekels on Goliath".'

Did you hear about the man who was chopping carrots with the Grim Reaper?
– He was dicing with death.

A terminally ill man woke up in a hospital bed and called for his doctor. 'Be honest with me, doc,' he said. 'How long have I got?'

'I'd be surprised if you survive the night,' replied the physician gloomily.

'Okay,' said the man. 'I'd like you to fetch me my lawyer.'

When the lawyer arrived, the man asked for the physician to stand on one side of the bed while the lawyer stood on the other. The man then closed his eyes.

After a few minutes, the physician asked him what he was thinking about.

The man replied: 'Jesus died with a thief on either side. I thought I'd check out the same way.'

On their first trip from the city, a pair of hunters were out in the woods when one of them suddenly collapsed. He didn't appear to be breathing and his eyes looked lifeless. The other hunter quickly called the emergency services on his mobile phone. He gasped to the operator: 'My friend is dead. What should I do?'

In a reassuring voice, the operator said: 'Okay, stay calm. I can help. First, let's make sure he's dead.'

The operator heard silence, then the sound of a gunshot. The hunter's voice came back on the line. 'Okay. Now what?'

Two men were riding down the road on a motorcycle. The driver was wearing a leather jacket with a broken zip and eventually he stopped to tell his pillion passenger: 'I can't drive any longer with the cold wind hitting me in my chest.' So he decided to put the jacket on backwards to guard against the onrushing wind chill.

They set off again but a mile further on he took

a corner too fast and smashed into a tree. A farmer who lived nearby was first on the scene.

Shortly afterwards a police car pulled up. Looking at the wreckage, the police officer asked the farmer: 'Are either of them showing any signs of life?'

'Well,' said the farmer, 'the first one was until I turned his head around the right way.'

A lawyer was reading out the will of a wealthy man to all of the people mentioned in the document.

'To you, my loving wife Susan who stood by me through thick and thin, I leave you the house and three million dollars. To my darling daughter Becky who looked after me when my health failed and never once complained, I leave you my yacht, the business and one million dollars. And to my brother Neville who argued with me constantly, hated my guts and thought that I would never mention him in my will . . . well you were wrong. Hi, Neville!'

A man went to the doctor for his annual physical. The man was shocked when the doctor told him: 'You've only got three weeks to live.'

'That can't be right!' said the man. 'I feel fine. Isn't

there anything that can be done?'

'Well,' said the doctor, 'you could try taking a mud bath every day.'

'And will that cure me?' asked the man hopefully.

'No, but it will get you used to the dirt.'

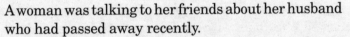

A woman was talking to her friends about her husband who had passed away recently.

'When he was on his deathbed, Edward told me that he had three envelopes in his desk drawer that would take care of all the arrangements. Well, he died shortly afterwards, so I opened the drawer, and there were the three envelopes, just like he had said.

'On the first envelope Edward had written "for the coffin". There were five thousand dollars in the envelope, so I bought him a nice coffin.

'On the second envelope Edward had written "for the expenses". There were four thousand dollars in that envelope, so I used the money to pay all the funeral bills.

'On the third envelope Edward had written "for the stone". There were three thousand dollars in that.'

Holding her hand out to her friends, she said: 'And isn't it beautiful?'

Eric was walking along the road when he saw a funeral procession approaching. Two hearses were followed by a man walking with a pitbull terrier on a lead. Behind the man and dog were about a hundred other men walking in single file.

Curious as to the nature of the procession, Eric asked the man with the dog: 'Excuse me, I don't wish to appear intrusive but could you tell me whose funeral this is?'

The man replied: 'The first hearse is for my wife. She died after my dog attacked her. And the second hearse is for my mother-in-law. She was trying to help my wife when the dog turned on her and savaged her to death, too.'

Eric thought for a moment and said: 'Is there any chance I could borrow your dog?'

Indicating the line of people behind him, the man said: 'Join the queue!'

Quasimodo placed an advert in a newspaper for an assistant bell ringer. There was one applicant for the post, but he had no arms.

'How will you be able to assist me?' asked Quasimodo.

'I'll show you,' replied the man who proceeded to run at the bell and strike it with his head.

'That's incredible!' exclaimed Quasimodo. 'Can you show me that again?'

'Sure,' said the man, and he ran at the bell again, but this time he missed the bell completely and fell to his death from the tower.

A crowd soon gathered around the corpse lying in the street. A police officer asked: 'Does anyone know who he is?'

Quasimodo said: 'I don't know his name, but his face rings a bell.'

Doctors and Nurses

A woman was asked to give a talk on the power of prayer to her local women's group. With her husband sitting in the audience, she recounted how they had turned to God when her husband suffered an unfortunate accident.

'Six months ago,' she began, 'my husband Keith was knocked off his bicycle and his scrotum was smashed. The pain was excruciating and the doctors didn't know if they could help him. They warned that our lives might never be the same again. Keith was unable to get close to either me or the children and every move caused him enormous discomfort. It meant we could no longer touch him around the scrotum.

'So we prayed that the doctors would be able to repair him. Fortunately our prayers were answered and they were able to piece together the crushed remnants of Keith's scrotum and wrap wire around it to hold it in place. They said he should make a complete recovery and regain full use of his scrotum.'

As the audience burst into spontaneous applause, a lone man walked up to the stage. He announced: 'Good afternoon. My name is Keith, and I just want to tell my wife once again that the word is "sternum".'

A woman went to the doctor's surgery where she was seen by one of the new young medics. But a few minutes later, she screamed, ran from the examination room in tears and hurried straight home.

A senior doctor witnessed the distressing scene and asked the young doctor what the problem was.

'I told her she was pregnant,' he said.

'What are you talking about?!' exclaimed the older doctor. 'Mrs Petty is seventy-three, she has two grown-up children and five grandchildren – and you told her she was pregnant?!'

'Well,' smiled the young doctor, 'it cured her hiccups though, didn't it?'

What does it mean when the doctor says you have six months to live?
– You have five months to pay.

A man went to the doctor to say he was having problems sleeping.

'Listen,' said the doctor, 'if you want to cure your insomnia, you're going to have to stop taking your troubles to bed with you.'

'I know,' said the man, 'but my wife refuses to sleep alone.'

A newspaper proprietor went to the doctor and said: 'Doctor, I think I'm suffering from anxiety. You see, my paper has lost a hundred thousand readers over the past year.'

'Okay,' said the doctor. 'I'll prescribe you some tablets.'

'Will they cure my anxiety?'

'No, but they'll improve your circulation.'

'Doctor, doctor, please hurry. My son swallowed a razor blade.'

'Don't panic. I'm coming right away. Have you done anything yet?'

'Yes, I shaved with the electric razor.'

'Doctor, doctor, I can't stop singing "Green Green Grass of Home".'

'Ah, you seem to be suffering from Tom Jones Syndrome.'

'Really. Is it common?'

'It's not unusual.'

One afternoon two doctors from India were having a heated discussion. 'I say it's spelled W-H-O-O-M,' said the first Indian doctor.

The second Indian doctor disagreed. 'No, it's W-H-O-M-B.'

An American nurse, who was passing, said: 'Actually you're both wrong. It's spelled W-O-M-B.'

'Thank you, nurse,' said one of the doctors, 'but we prefer to settle this argument among ourselves.

Besides, we don't think you are in a position to describe the sound of an elephant passing wind under water.'

'Doctor, doctor, my wife has lost her voice. What should I do to help her get it back?'

'Try coming home at three o'clock in the morning.'

'Doctor, doctor, I can't get to sleep.'

'Try sitting on the edge of the bed. You'll soon drop off.'

A wealthy businessman injured his leg in a weekend skiing accident. By the time he got home on the Saturday night, his leg was badly swollen and he was struggling to walk, so he called his doctor at home. The doctor advised soaking it in hot water, but this caused the leg to swell up even more.

Seeing him limping in agony, the businessman's maid said: 'It's probably not my place because after all I'm only a humble maid, but I always thought it was better to use cold water, rather than hot, to reduce swelling.'

So he took her advice, switched to cold water, and the swelling quickly went down.

The following afternoon he called his doctor again to complain. 'What am I paying you for?' he demanded. 'Your advice was useless. You told me to soak my leg in hot water, and it got worse. My maid told me to use cold water, and it got better.'

'Really?' said the doctor. 'I don't understand it; my maid said hot water.'

'Doctor, doctor, I think I'm a dog.'
'How long have you had these symptoms?'
'Ever since I was a puppy.'

A woman went to the doctor. After examining her, the doctor said: 'I'm not sure what it is. You either have a bad cold or you're pregnant.'

'I must be pregnant,' said the woman. 'I don't know anyone who could have given me a cold.'

A patient went to see a doctor.

The doctor asked: 'Do you smoke?'

'No.'

'Do you drink?'

'No.'

'Do you eat fast food?'

'No.'

'Don't worry. I'm sure I'll find something.'

Two strangers – a man and a woman – were drinking and chatting together in a bar, and after a while they realized they were both doctors. They got on so well that after about an hour the man said: 'Why don't we go back to your place? We can have some fun. No strings attached.'

The woman doctor agreed, and they went back to her apartment. While he lay on the bed, she went into the bathroom and started scrubbing and cleaning herself meticulously. This went on for about ten minutes. Finally she emerged and they had sex.

Afterwards he said: 'You're a surgeon, aren't you?'

'Yes,' she replied. 'How did you know?'

'I could tell by the way you scrubbed up before we started.'

'Yes, I suppose that was a giveaway,' she agreed. 'And you're an anaesthetist, aren't you?'

'Yes, I am,' said the man, surprised. 'How did you know?'

The woman answered: 'Because I didn't feel a thing.'

'Doctor, doctor, I think I'm suffering from déjà vu.'

'Didn't I see you yesterday?'

A man walked into the doctor's office with a lettuce leaf sticking out of his ear.

'That's strange,' said the doctor.

The man said: 'That's just the tip of the iceberg.'

At the height of her career, a famous artist began to lose her eyesight. Afraid that it might wreck her work, she consulted a leading eye doctor, and following several months of delicate surgery her eyesight was restored.

She was so grateful that she offered to repaint the doctor's office in her own highly individual style. The finished work included a huge eye painted on one wall.

At a press conference to unveil the new artwork, the doctor was asked: 'What was your first reaction on seeing your newly painted office, especially that large eye on the wall?'

The eye doctor replied: 'I said to myself, "Thank goodness I'm not a gynaecologist!"'

'Doctor, doctor, I've got a cricket ball stuck in my ear.'

'How's that?'

'Oh, don't start . . . '

A doctor told his patient: 'There's good news and bad news.'

'Tell me the bad news first,' said the patient nervously.

'Well, I have the results of your tests and I'm afraid you have less than two weeks to live.'

The patient's heart sank. 'So what's the good news?'

The doctor said: 'Did you notice that sexy blonde on reception? I'm dating her.'

A man went to the doctor's, complaining of feeling generally unwell. The doctor gave him a thorough examination and was amazed to find hundreds of dollar bills stuffed in the patient's ears.

When he had finished counting them, the doctor said: 'There was exactly one thousand, nine hundred and fifty dollars in there.'

'That figures,' said the man. 'I knew I wasn't feeling two grand.'

A man went to the doctor and said: 'Doctor, can you cure my sleepwalking?'

'Try these,' the doctor advised, handing him a small box.

'Are they sleeping pills?'

'No, they're tin tacks. Sprinkle them on the floor.'

A patient told his doctor: 'Those pills you gave me are working fine but there's just one problem: they make me walk like a crab.'

'Ah,' said the doctor. 'Those will be the side effects.'

A woman accompanied her sick husband to the doctor's office. After examining him, the doctor called the wife into his office alone. He told her: 'I'm afraid your husband is suffering from an extremely serious disease, coupled with severe stress. If you don't follow my instructions for his care, he will die. Each morning, you must make him a healthy breakfast. For lunch make him a nutritious meal, and for dinner cook him whatever he asks for. Above all, he must not do any chores around the house nor must he be subjected to anything stressful. You must wait on him at all times, attending to his every need. If you can do this for the next eighteen months, I think your husband will pull through.'

As she left the office and closed the door behind her, her husband asked anxiously: 'What did the doctor say?'

She replied: 'He says you're going to die.'

Drunks

A drunk was driving the wrong way down a one-way street when a police officer pulled him over.

'Didn't you see the arrows?' asked the officer.

'Arrows?' repeated the driver in a slurred voice. 'I didn't even see the Indians!'

A man whispered to the bartender: 'I got so drunk last night, I ended up snogging my best friend.'

'That must have been really embarrassing,' said the bartender.

'It was,' said the man. 'I could hardly face taking him for a walk this morning.'

Late one night, a drunk was crawling around on his hands and knees beneath a street light, obviously searching for something. A passer-by offered to help.

'What have you lost?' he asked.

'My watch,' replied the drunk. 'It fell off when I tripped over the kerb.'

The passer-by helped him search but after fifteen minutes there was still no sign of the missing watch.

'Where exactly did you trip?' asked the passer-by.

'About two hundred yards back there,' answered the drunk.

'So why are you looking for your watch here if you lost it two hundred yards up the street?'

The drunk said: 'Because the lighting is much better here.'

A drunk phoned police to report that thieves had been in his car. 'I don't believe it!' he groaned: 'They've stolen the radio, the glove compartment, the dashboard, the steering wheel, the brake pedal, even the accelerator.'

Five minutes later, the phone at the police station rang again. It was the same drunk. 'Sorry,' he slurred. 'I just realized I got in the back seat by mistake.'

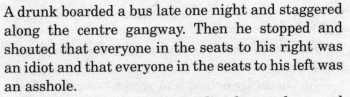

A drunk boarded a bus late one night and staggered along the centre gangway. Then he stopped and shouted that everyone in the seats to his right was an idiot and that everyone in the seats to his left was an asshole.

An angry passenger immediately stood up and said: 'How dare you! I'm not an idiot!'

The drunk said: 'So move to the other side.'

A drunk stumbled across a baptismal service one Sunday afternoon down by the river. He proceeded to stand in the water next to the preacher.

After a minute or so, the preacher turned to him and said: 'Brother, are you ready to find Jesus?'

'Yes, I am,' replied the drunk unsteadily.

The preacher then pushed the drunk's head under water before pulling him back up. 'Have you found Jesus?' he asked.

'No, I haven't,' said the drunk.

The preacher then held him under water for

a longer period before bringing him back up and asking: 'Now have you found Jesus?'

Wiping the water from his eyes, the drunk replied: 'No, I haven't.'

So the preacher held the drunk's head forcefully under water for over thirty seconds before dragging him back up and bellowing: 'Have you found Jesus yet?'

Spitting fountains of water from his mouth, the drunk steadied himself and said to the preacher: 'Are you sure this is where he fell in?'

Did you hear about the guy who got drunk and collapsed in a heap beside the bar?
– It caused a major delay in the gymnastics competition.

A stout woman walked into a bar carrying a duck under her arm. A drunk sitting nearby called out: 'Where did you get that pig?'

'It's not a pig,' snapped the woman. 'It's a duck.'

The drunk said: 'I was talking to the duck!'

Why did John call his father-in-law the exorcist?
– Because whenever he visited he rid the house of spirits.

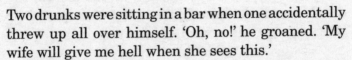

Two drunks were sitting in a bar when one accidentally threw up all over himself. 'Oh, no!' he groaned. 'My wife will give me hell when she sees this.'

'Don't worry,' said the second drunk. 'I'll tell you what to do. Put twenty dollars in your shirt pocket, and when your wife asks what the money's for, tell her that a man threw up over you and gave you twenty dollars to get your shirt cleaned.'

'Hey, that's a great idea,' said the first drunk.

When he returned home later in the evening, his wife was predictably angry. 'Look at the state of you!' she yelled. 'You're covered in vomit!'

'It wasn't my fault,' said the drunk. 'A man threw up over me and gave me twenty dollars to have my shirt cleaned. Look, here's the money.' And with that he lifted the cash from his shirt pocket.

'But there's forty dollars here!' said the wife.

'Ah, yes,' replied the drunk. 'I forget to mention, he pooped in my underpants, too.'

A drunk fell down the steps of the Hilton Hotel, stumbled to a waiting cab and, climbing in, said to the driver: 'Take me to the Hilton.'

'We're already there,' replied the taxi driver.

'That's great,' said the drunk. 'But next time, don't drive so fast.'

After a night on the town, a husband lurched home at three o'clock in the morning. Just as he stepped through the front door, the cuckoo clock started and cuckooed three times. Realizing that the clock would almost certainly wake his wife, he cuckooed another nine times.

The next morning his wife asked him what time he had arrived home.

'Twelve o'clock,' he answered.

When she didn't argue, he was sure his deception had worked. But then she added: 'By the way we really must get a new cuckoo clock. Last night it cuckooed three times, said "damn", cuckooed another four times, belched, cuckooed another three times, cleared its throat, cuckooed twice more and giggled!'

A police officer stopped a drunk who was staggering along the street at five o'clock in the morning.

The officer said: 'Can you explain why you're out at this hour?'

The drunk replied: 'If I could, I'd be home by now!'

A drunk staggered down to hotel reception and demanded a change of room. He was so insistent that the receptionist decided to call the manager.

'What exactly is the problem?' asked the manager.

'I want another room,' said the drunk.

'But I see you're in room 562. That's one of the best rooms in the hotel.'

'I don't care,' said the drunk. 'I want another room.'

'Very well, sir. Our aim is always to please our guests. So if you're adamant, we can move you from 562 to 575. But would you mind telling me what you don't like about your room?'

'Well,' said the drunk, 'for a start, it's on fire.'

A police officer saw a drunk wandering home in a smart neighbourhood. Suspicious because the man was struggling to get his key in the door lock, the officer approached him and asked: 'Are you sure this is your house, sir?'

'Absolutely,' said the drunk. 'And if you follow me in, I'll prove it to you.'

As they entered the living room, the drunk said: 'See that couch? That's mine, that is. And see that piano? That's mine, too.'

Then he led the officer gingerly upstairs. 'See,' slurred the drunk. 'This is my bedroom. See the bed? That's mine. See the woman lying in the bed? That's my wife. And see the guy lying next to her . . . ?'

'Yes . . .' said the officer, more suspicious than ever.

'Well, that's me!'

Two men were sitting in a bar when one turned to the other and said: 'You see that guy over there? Don't you think he looks just like me?'

The man went over to his doppelgänger and said: 'Excuse me, but I couldn't help noticing that you're a dead ringer for me.'

'You're right, I do look like you.'

'Where are you from?'

'Dublin.'

'Me, too.'

'Which street?'

'Ballymount Drive.'

'Ballymount Drive? That's incredible! That's my street, too. What number?'

'Sixty-three.'

'Sixty-three! I don't believe it! Me, too. What are your parents' names?'

'Pat and Josephine.'

'Pat and Josephine! Unbelievable! So are mine!'

Just then the bartenders changed shifts. 'Anything much happened?' asked the new bartender.

'Not really,' said the old one. 'Oh, except the O'Malley twins are drunk again.'

The Inebriation Scale

0. Stone cold sober. Brain as sharp as an army bayonet.

1. Still sober. Pleasure senses activated. Feeling of well-being.

2. Beer warming up head. Barmaid complimented

on choice of blouse/barman complimented on nice shirt.

3. Nicely mellow. Barmaid complimented on choice of bra/barman complimented on his boxers.

4. Have brilliant discussion with guy at bar. Devise foolproof scheme for winning lottery. Agree that people are same world over except for bloody French.

5. Feel like a demigod. Map out rest of life on beer mat. Realize that everybody loves you. Phone parents and tell them you love them. Phone girlfriend/boyfriend to tell them you love them and they still have an amazing arse.

6. Send drinks over to attractive woman/man on night out with friends. Start kissing total strangers.

7. Some slurring of words. Offer to buy drinks for everyone in bar. Lots of people say yes. Go round hugging them one by one. Fall over. Get up.

8. Headache kicks in. Beer tastes off. Send it back. Beer comes back tasting same. Say, 'That's much better.' Fight nausea by trying to play poker machine for ten minutes before seeing 'Out of order' sign.

9. Some doubling of vision. Room suddenly full of identical twins. Offer to have someone's baby. Become very loud. Fall over. Get up. Fall over. Impale head on corner of table. Fail to notice gaping head wound.

10. Speech no longer possible. Eventually manage to find door. Sit and take stock. Realize you are sitting in pub cellar, having taken a wrong turn. Vomit. Pass out.

11. Put in taxi by somebody. Vomit on back seat. Taxi driver throws you out of cab after relieving you of a hundred dollars for cleaning bill. Fall in hedge. Stagger home. Accidentally kick over milk bottle on front step, waking all neighbours. At ninth attempt, successfully get key in door. Slump in hallway, generally pleased at way evening has gone. Pass out again.

Farming

A city family bought a farm in the country, where they planned to raise cattle. A friend came to visit one weekend and asked if the ranch had a name.

'Well,' said the would-be cattleman, 'to be honest we've had a few arguments over names. I wanted to call the ranch Bar-K; my wife preferred Lindy-M; one son liked the Happy-J; and my other son wanted the Busy-B. So as a compromise we've called it the Bar-K-Lindy-M-Happy-J-Busy-B Ranch.'

'I see,' said the friend. 'But tell me, where are all your cattle?'

'So far, none have survived the branding.'

An old farmer had dedicated his life to collecting tractors. By the age of seventy he had built up a collection of hundreds of tractors from all over the world, but then he began to tire of the hobby. He had to spend hours each day cleaning them, ensuring that they were in immaculate condition, but eventually he realized there were better things he could be doing with his time. So he decided to sell his collection to an enthusiast from Iowa.

To discuss the terms of the sale, the farmer arranged to meet the buyer in a local bar popular with farming folk. The air was thick with pipe smoke but the farmer enjoyed talking to the buyer about the tractors that had once been his great passion. After an hour or so, he asked the buyer if he wanted another beer.

'That would be good,' said the buyer, 'but would you mind if we went someplace else? The air in here is so smoky I can hardly breathe.'

'There's no need for us to leave,' said the farmer. 'Here, watch this.'

With that, the farmer took a deep breath and sucked in every last particle of smoke from the room. Then he leaned out of the window and blew the smoke away.

'How did you manage that?' asked the buyer.

'It was easy,' said the farmer. 'Remember, I'm an ex-tractor fan.'

Before hurrying into town on business, a farmer said to his wife: 'Oh, I nearly forgot. That guy will be along this afternoon to impregnate one of the cows. I've hung a nail by the correct stall so you'll know which one I want him to impregnate. Are you clear with that?'

The wife, who knew precious little about farming, nodded hesitantly.

That afternoon, the inseminator arrived, and the wife, as instructed, led him out to the barn and directly to the stall with the nail.

'This is the cow right here,' she said.

'What's the nail for?' asked the inseminator.

The wife shrugged and replied: 'I guess it's to hang up your pants.'

A city guy was visiting a small farm in the country, where he saw the farmer feed his pigs in a most peculiar way. The farmer would lift the pig up to an apple tree and allow the pig to eat the fruit straight from the tree. He would then move the pig from one apple to another until it had eaten enough before starting the process all over again with the next pig.

After observing this routine for half an hour, the city guy felt he had to say something. 'The way you feed your pigs is terribly inefficient,' he said. 'Just think of the time that would be saved if you simply shook the apples off the tree and let the pigs eat them from the ground.'

The farmer shrugged his shoulders and replied: 'What's time to a pig?'

A man was driving along a country road when he saw a farmer standing in the middle of a large field. The farmer wasn't doing anything and simply appeared to be gazing into the distance.

The driver stopped his car and called out: 'What are you doing?'

'I'm trying to win a Nobel Prize,' replied the farmer.

'I don't understand.'

'Well,' explained the farmer, 'I heard they give the Nobel Prize to people who are out standing in their field.'

What did the farmer say to the goat that wouldn't reproduce?
– You must be kidding.

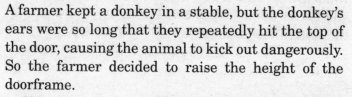

A farmer kept a donkey in a stable, but the donkey's ears were so long that they repeatedly hit the top of the door, causing the animal to kick out dangerously. So the farmer decided to raise the height of the doorframe.

He spent all day toiling away with his hacksaw. Seeing that he was struggling to complete the task, his neighbour suggested: 'Instead of lifting the doorframe, wouldn't it be easier if you simply dug out the ground in the doorway and made it deeper?'

'Don't be stupid,' said the farmer. 'It's the donkey's ears that are too long, not his legs!'

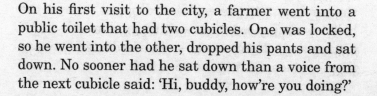

On his first visit to the city, a farmer went into a public toilet that had two cubicles. One was locked, so he went into the other, dropped his pants and sat down. No sooner had he sat down than a voice from the next cubicle said: 'Hi, buddy, how're you doing?'

The farmer was a bit freaked out by this but, not wishing to appear rude, he answered: 'Not too bad, thanks.'

There was a short pause and then he heard the voice again. 'So what are you up to?'

The farmer wasn't sure whether or not to answer but reluctantly replied: 'Just having a poop. You?'

Then he heard the voice for a third time. 'Sorry, buddy, I'll have to call you back. Some idiot in the next cubicle is answering everything I say.'

While out walking one day, two men came across an abandoned well. Curious as to how deep it was, they threw a stone down the well and waited for the sound of it hitting the bottom. But they heard nothing.

So they found a larger rock and threw that down the well. Still they heard nothing.

They clearly needed something bigger and after a quick search of the surrounding area, they found a railway sleeper. Summoning every ounce of their combined strength, they managed to carry the heavy sleeper across to the well and dropped it down the hole. As they stood back waiting for the sound of it hitting the bottom, a goat suddenly darted between them and leaped into the open well.

The men were still recovering from the shock when a farmer appeared.

'Have either of you seen a goat?' he asked.

'Yes,' they said. 'One just jumped down that well.'

'No, that couldn't have been my goat,' said the farmer. 'Mine was tethered to a railway sleeper.'

A farmer who looked after baby animals was stunned by the brutal murder of a piglet. He was determined to find the culprit but the only witness to the killing was a hare from an adjoining field. Since the hare was unable to speak, the farmer lined up his four prime suspects – a cow, a horse, a young goat and a duck – and staged an ID parade. 'Right, hare,' he said, 'I want you to pick out the animal that killed my piglet.'

The hare hopped up and down the line, checking each animal, before finally hopping forward two paces and stopping in front of the young goat.

'It wasn't me! It wasn't me!' protested the goat.

The farmer shook his head and said: 'Hare's looking at you, kid.'

Fish and Fishing

Put in charge of his baby sister for the day, a young boy decided to take her fishing. But when his parents returned home, he was in a bad mood.

'I'm never taking my sister fishing again,' he told his mother. 'I didn't catch a thing!'

'Never mind,' said his mother. 'Next time I'm sure she'll be quiet and not scare the fish away.'

'It wasn't that,' said the boy. 'She ate all the bait!'

A man rang his wife at home and said: 'Honey, I've been asked to go fishing at a lake up in Canada with my boss and a few of his friends, leaving tonight. We'll be away for the rest of the week. I know it's short notice, but it's a great opportunity for me to get that promotion I've been chasing. So will you pack me enough clothes for the rest of the week and set out my rod and tackle box. I'll drop by and collect everything on my way from the office. Oh, and by the way, please pack my new blue silk pyjamas.'

The wife thought the last request sounded highly suspicious but nevertheless she did as he asked.

When he returned from his trip away, she asked him how it had gone.

'I'm a bit tired,' he said, 'but otherwise it was fine.'

'And did you catch many fish?'

'Oh, yes, plenty,' he said. 'More than anyone else. But why didn't you pack my new blue silk pyjamas like I asked?'

'I did,' she replied. 'They were in your tackle box.'

A mother said to her young son: 'Have you put fresh water in the goldfish's bowl?'

'I don't need to,' said the boy. 'He hasn't finished the last lot yet.'

A game warden spotted a man carrying two buckets of fish away from a lake. 'Hey, buddy,' he called out. 'Do you have a licence to catch those fish?'

The man said: 'No, but you don't understand. These are my pet fish.'

'Pet fish?' replied the warden in disbelief.

'Yes, that's right. Every night I take these fish down to the lake and let them swim around for a while. Then when I whistle, they jump back into their buckets and I take them home.'

'I've never heard such a load of garbage,' said the warden. 'Fish can't do that!'

The man thought for a second before suggesting: 'If you don't believe me, I'll show you.'

'I can't wait to see this!' said the warden mockingly.

So the man poured the fish into the lake and stood and waited. After several minutes, the game warden turned to him and said: 'Well?'

'Well what?' asked the man.

'When are you going to call them back?'

'Call who back?'

'The fish!' yelled the warden.

'What fish?'

Two sardines were big tennis fans. 'Let's go to Wimbledon this year,' said one.

'How would we get there?' asked the other.

'On the London Underground, of course.'

'What, and get packed in like commuters?'

Four married men went fishing. After they had been out on the lake for about an hour, the first man said: 'You have no idea what I had to do so I could come fishing this weekend. I had to promise my wife that I'd redecorate the living room and hallway next weekend.'

'That's nothing,' said the second man. 'I had to promise my wife that I'd build a new deck for the pool area.'

'You both have it easy!' said the third man. 'I had to promise my wife that I'd buy her a new kitchen and pay for her to go clothes shopping with her friends next month.'

They continued fishing until they realized that the fourth man had remained strangely silent. Eventually they turned to him and said: 'So what did you have to do in order to come fishing this weekend?'

'Nothing much,' said the fourth man. 'I simply set my alarm for 5.30 a.m. When it went off, I nudged my wife and said: "Fishing or sex?" And she said: "Wear a sweater."'

How did the police know that the man eaten by a shark had dandruff?
– They found his head and shoulders on the beach.

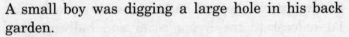

A small boy was digging a large hole in his back garden.

'What are you doing, Tim?' asked the man next door, peering over the fence.

The boy said: 'My goldfish died and I'm burying him.'

'That's a big hole just for a goldfish,' said the neighbour.

The boy replied: 'That's because he's inside your cat.'

Why don't oysters give to charity?
– They're shellfish.

158

A man went into a pet shop and asked: 'Can I buy a goldfish?'

'Certainly, sir,' said the sales assistant. 'Do you want an aquarium?'

The man said: 'I don't care what star sign it is.'

A couple went on vacation to a fishing resort. The husband liked to fish first thing in the morning while his wife was just happy reading. One day, the husband returned to their cabin after several hours on the lake and decided to take a midday nap. Although unfamiliar with the lake, the wife fancied a spot of fresh air and decided to take the boat out. She motored out a short distance, anchored the boat, and then continued reading her book in the tranquil setting.

Within minutes, a game warden had arrived on the scene in his boat. 'Good day, ma'am,' he said. 'What are you doing?'

'Reading a book,' she replied.

'You're in a restricted fishing area.'

'Look, officer,' she protested, 'I'm not fishing, I'm reading.'

As he glanced at the boat, he said: 'Yes, but you have all the equipment. For all I know, you could start at any moment. I'll have to take you in and write you up.'

'If you do that,' said the woman, 'I'll have to charge you with sexual assault.'

'What do you mean?' said the warden. 'I haven't laid a finger on you!'

'That's true,' said the woman. 'But you have all the equipment. For all I know, you could start at any moment.'

'Have a nice day, ma'am,' grumbled the warden as he left.

It was a quiet day on the ark, so a bored Noah told his wife that he was going fishing. He collected all his equipment and set off, but thirty minutes later he was back, still complaining that he was bored.

'What are you doing back so soon?' asked his wife. 'If you're that bored, why did you stop fishing after only half an hour?'

Noah said: 'I only had two worms.'

Food and Drink

While browsing around a department store, a man spotted a Thermos flask. He had never seen one before, so he asked the sales assistant what it did. The assistant replied: 'It keeps hot things hot and cold things cold.'

Impressed, the man bought one. The next day, he took the Thermos into work and showed it off to a colleague.

'Look at this,' he said. 'It's called a Thermos flask. It keeps hot things hot and cold things cold.'

'What have you got in there?' asked his workmate.

The man said: 'Two cups of coffee and a choc ice.'

Did you hear about the pizza deliveryman who was found lying in the street covered in anchovies, spicy beef, pineapple and pepperoni?
– The police say he topped himself.

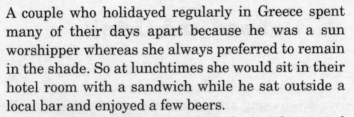

A couple who holidayed regularly in Greece spent many of their days apart because he was a sun worshipper whereas she always preferred to remain in the shade. So at lunchtimes she would sit in their hotel room with a sandwich while he sat outside a local bar and enjoyed a few beers.

One day he stayed away a little longer than usual for lunch and when he returned to the room, she was furious.

'Where have you been?' she moaned. 'I've been dying of thirst here. What do you think I am, a bloody camel?'

'Why didn't you go to the pool bar and buy some water?' he said. 'It's only just over there.'

'You know I can't go out in the sun in the middle of the day. Anyway, now you're finally here, I want you to go and get me a bottle. But remember, it must be still water. I don't want any of that sparkling stuff.'

'Okay. I'll be sure to get still water.'

So he set off for the pool bar and returned a few minutes later carrying a bottle of water.

'Is it still water?' she demanded.

'Of course it's still water,' he replied wearily. 'Who do you think I am, bloody Jesus?'

What's smelly, round and laughs?
– A tickled onion.

A customer in a restaurant asked: 'How do you prepare the chicken?'

'We don't,' said the waiter. 'We just tell it straight that it's going to die.'

What do you get if you cross a strong onion with a goat?
– Garlic butter.

A man walked into a branch of Starbucks and ordered a coffee. But when he tried to drink it, he found that instead of coffee, his cup contained a pair of beige cotton trousers.

'Excuse me,' he said to the waiter. 'This isn't what I ordered.'

'It must have been,' said the waiter, shrugging his shoulders and walking away. 'We don't make mistakes.'

Seething with indignation, the customer summoned the manager and said: 'This isn't what I ordered. I want coffee, not trousers.'

'Listen, sir,' replied the manager. 'It is exactly what you ordered – a cup o' chinos.'

What's the difference between roast beef and pea soup?
– Anyone can roast beef.

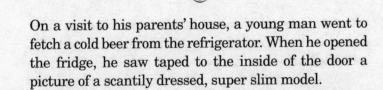

On a visit to his parents' house, a young man went to fetch a cold beer from the refrigerator. When he opened the fridge, he saw taped to the inside of the door a picture of a scantily dressed, super slim model.

'What's with the picture?' he asked his mother.

She explained: 'I put it up there to remind me not to overeat.'

'Is it working?'

'Yes and no. I've lost fifteen pounds, but your father has gained twenty!'

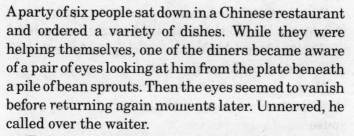

A party of six people sat down in a Chinese restaurant and ordered a variety of dishes. While they were helping themselves, one of the diners became aware of a pair of eyes looking at him from the plate beneath a pile of bean sprouts. Then the eyes seemed to vanish before returning again moments later. Unnerved, he called over the waiter.

'Excuse me, waiter,' he said, 'but I think there's a pair of eyes that keep looking at me from that plate of food. You can't see them at the moment but they'll be back very soon.'

'Don't worry, sir,' said the waiter. 'That's the Peking duck.'

A man walked into a fish and chip shop and said: 'I'll have fish and chips twice.'

The guy behind the counter said: 'I heard you the first time!'

What's white, light and sugary and swings from trees?
– A meringue-utan.

A man sat down for a three-course meal in a restaurant. First, the waitress brought him a bowl of soup but he couldn't help noticing that her thumb was sticking in the soup.

Next, she brought him chicken supreme, but again he noticed that her thumb was sticking in the sauce.

Finally for dessert he ordered hot apple pie, and once again her thumb was sticking in his food.

'Look!' he said in exasperation, 'I wasn't going to mention it but every time you serve me, your thumb is stuck in my food.'

'Yes, I'm sorry about that,' said the waitress, 'but you see, my thumb has an infection. My doctor says I need to keep it in a warm moist place.'

Disgusted, the customer snapped: 'Well, why don't you stick it up your ass!'

The waitress replied: 'Where do you think I've been putting it when I'm in the kitchen?'

A woman baked two cakes to sell at her village fete – one for five dollars, the other for ten dollars. A man soon expressed an interest in buying one and, pointing at the ten-dollar cake, asked her: 'What type of cake is that?'

The woman replied: 'That's Madeira cake.'

An Englishman ordered the soup of the day in a New York restaurant. When the waitress brought it to his table, the Englishman eyed it suspiciously.

'What is it?' he asked.

'It's bean soup,' she replied.

'I don't care what it's been,' he said. 'I want to know what it is now!'

A woman was looking through the frozen turkeys at a supermarket but couldn't find one big enough to feed her family.

She asked a stock boy: 'Do these turkeys get any bigger?'

'No, ma'am,' he replied. 'They're dead.'

A middle-aged man was sitting quietly in a roadside cafe when three rough bikers strode in. The first strolled over to the man and stubbed a cigarette into his lunch. Then the second spat in the man's coffee. Finally the third biker picked up the man's lunch and, roaring with laughter, threw it onto the floor. Without saying a word, the man got up and left.

'He wasn't much of a man, was he?' sneered one of the bikers to the waitress.

'Not much of a driver either,' she said, glancing out of the window. 'He's just backed his truck over three motorcycles.'

As he passed by a seafood restaurant, a man saw a sign in the window saying, 'Lobster Tails Three Dollars.'

Sensing a bargain, he went inside and asked the waitress why they were so cheap. 'They must be very short tails for that price,' he suggested.

'No,' replied the waitress. 'They're normal length.'

'Then they must be fairly old.'

'No, they're fresh today.'

'There must be something wrong with them . . .'

'No, they're just regular lobster tails.'

'Okay,' said the man. 'For three dollars I'll have one.'

So the waitress took his money, sat him down and said: 'Once upon a time there was a big red lobster . . .'

A chicken and a pig were drinking together in a bar one evening when the chicken said: 'Why don't we go into business together? We could open a ham and egg restaurant.'

'Not so fast,' said the pig. 'For you, it's just a day's work. For me, it's a matter of life and death.'

Fred Astaire and Ginger Rogers were dining in a five-star New York City hotel, and both made a point of dressing for the occasion. Ginger looked resplendent in a ball gown and diamond tiara while Fred wore his smartest morning suit. However the evening was marred when the waiter bringing their desserts tripped and covered Fred from head to toe in treacle sponge.

'I'm most terribly sorry, Mr Astaire,' said the waiter.

'So you ought to be,' replied Fred. 'Look at the state of me! I've got pudding on my top hat, pudding on my white tie, pudding on my tails.'

Genies

A married couple were playing golf when the husband's wayward tee shot smashed through the window of an old house that adjoined the course. Seeking to retrieve his ball, they walked over to the house and, finding the back door open, ventured hesitantly inside. They called out: 'Is anyone there?' 'Yes, come in,' replied a voice.

Inside they found glass everywhere, a broken bottle on the floor and a man sitting on the couch.

'Are you the people who broke my window?' asked the man.

'Yes, sorry about that,' said the husband.

'There's no need to apologize,' said the man. 'In

fact, you've done me a favour. You see, I'm a genie who was trapped in that bottle until your wayward shot released me. So I want to thank you, and as a fully-fledged genie I'm allowed to grant you three wishes. I'd like to grant you one wish each and, if you don't mind, I'll keep the last wish for myself as compensation for being stuck in that bottle for the past ten years.'

'Fantastic,' said the husband. 'My wish is to have a fleet of top-of-the-range sports cars.'

'No problem,' said the genie. 'And what is your wish, madam?'

'My wish', said the wife, 'is simply to own all the clothes I've ever dreamed of but have never been able to afford.'

'Consider it done,' said the genie. Turning to the husband, he continued: 'And now for my wish. Because I've been trapped in that damn bottle, I haven't had sex for ages. So if you don't mind, I'd like to sleep with your wife.'

The husband thought for a moment and replied: 'I don't see why not. It seems only fair. After all, we are going to be getting all those cars and clothes. Is that okay with you, darling?'

'I guess so,' agreed the wife.

So the genie took her upstairs and ravished her for four and a half hours. When he was finally satisfied, he rolled over, looked at her and said: 'Tell me, how old is your husband?'

'Forty-one,' she replied.

'And he still believes in genies?'

An Englishman and a Scotsman were walking in the country when they came across a lamp. They instinctively rubbed the lamp and out popped a genie.

'Thank you so much,' said the genie. 'I'm free at last. And to show my gratitude I'll grant you both one wish.'

The Englishman said: 'I'm fed up with the Scots always coming into England. I wish there was a huge wall around England to keep the Scots out.'

'Very well,' said the genie and POOF it was done.

Then the Scotsman turned to the genie and said: 'Tell me about this wall.'

The genie said: 'It's three hundred feet high and a quarter of a mile thick. Nobody can get in and nobody can get out.'

'Right,' said the Scotsman, 'fill it with water.'

Following a violent storm, an old man and a younger man were swept out to sea in a rowing boat. They drifted for two weeks and had given up hope of ever seeing land again. Then under a tarpaulin the old man discovered a gold lamp. In a last, desperate gesture he gave it a rub and to his amazement a genie appeared.

'I'm afraid I can only grant you one wish,' said the genie.

'That's okay,' said the old man, gasping with thirst. 'I want you turn the entire ocean into beer.'

'Your wish is my command,' said the genie. He clicked his fingers and immediately the salt water changed into beer. Then the genie vanished.

The younger man looked at his friend in disgust. 'Fancy wasting our wish on turning the sea into beer! You silly old fool! Now we'll have to pee in the boat!'

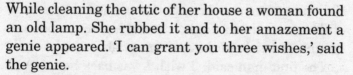

While cleaning the attic of her house a woman found an old lamp. She rubbed it and to her amazement a genie appeared. 'I can grant you three wishes,' said the genie.

The woman said: 'But I have everything in life that I could ever need.'

'You don't want these wishes to go to waste,' replied the genie. 'Try and think of something.'

'Well, I suppose a new dining-room table would be nice. I've had the old one for over forty years.'

The genie immediately produced a brand new

dining-room table. 'And for your second wish?'

'Well,' said the woman, 'it would be handy to have a new car so that I can get to church more easily.'

The genie immediately produced a new car. 'And what is your third wish?'

After giving the matter careful thought, the woman said: 'I suppose there's not much use having a new car without somebody to share it with. Is it in your power to turn my dear old cat into a handsome young man?'

The cat was immediately turned into a handsome hunk. The young man strolled over to the woman and said: 'I bet you're sorry you had me neutered now.'

Three men had been stranded on a desert island for ten years when one day a bottle washed ashore. One of the men rubbed the bottle and a genie appeared. He granted each of the men one wish.

The first man said: 'I wish I was back home.' And POOF he disappeared.

The second man said: 'I also wish I was back home with my family.' And POOF he disappeared.

Alone on the island, the third man suddenly felt very lonely and sighed: 'I wish my two friends were back on this island with me.' And POOF the other two men reappeared on the island.

While playing tennis, a man found an old bottle lying in the corner of the court. As he rubbed it clean, a genie appeared and granted him three wishes. However to the genie's surprise, the man said: 'It's very kind of you, but there's really nothing I need. Please give the wishes to someone else.'

However the genie decided to reward the man for his generosity by granting him three things without him even knowing. 'What does every man want?' the genie thought to himself. 'I know: money, power and sex. I'll give him all three.'

Two weeks later, the genie met the man again at the tennis court. 'How's it going?' asked the genie.

'Things couldn't be better,' said the man. 'Last week I raised over one million dollars and gave the most invigorating talk of my career. I feel as if I finally have real influence among my peers.'

'That's great,' said the genie. 'And if you don't mind me asking, how's your sex life?'

'Fantastic,' said the man. 'I've had two women in the last two weeks.'

'Only two?' said the genie, disappointed. 'That's not very good.'

The man said: 'It is if you're a priest in a small parish!'

GOOD, BAD, WORSE

Good: Your boyfriend's exercising.
Bad: So he'll fit in your clothes.

Good: You come home for a quickie.
Bad: Your wife walks in.

Good: Your mother-in-law's going home.
Bad: To put her house up for sale.

Good: Your neighbour exercises in the nude.
Bad: He weighs 350 pounds.

Good: Your girlfriend's got long, soft, dark hair.
Bad: On her top lip.

Good: Your wife meets you at the door naked.
Bad: She's coming home.

Good: You get tickets to the theatre.
Bad: It's performance art.

Bad: Your wife wants a divorce.
Worse: She's a lawyer.

Bad: You find a porn movie in your son's room.
Worse: You're in it.

Bad: Your children are sexually active.
Worse: With each other.

Bad: Your son's involved in Satanism.
Worse: As a sacrifice.

Bad: Your husband's a cross-dresser.
Worse: He looks better than you.

Bad: You're arrested for flashing.
Worse: The victim decides it's not worth pressing charges.

Good: You give the birds and bees talk to your eight-year-old daughter.
Bad: She keeps interrupting.
Worse: With corrections.

Good: The mailman's early.
Bad: He's wearing camouflage gear and carrying a sub-machine gun.
Worse: You put nothing in his Christmas box.

Good: Your wife's kinky.
Bad: With the neighbours.
Worse: All of them.

Health and Fitness

After going to the hospital for what he thought was merely a routine check-up, a man was devastated to learn that he had the rare deadly disease B55. The doctor told him that he had just one week to live.

Determined to make the most of his final week of life, he decided to fit in as many activities as possible, including take his wife out to bingo one evening. There, he entered the prize draw game. First, he got one line and won fifteen thousand dollars; then he got two lines and won a car; and finally he got a full house and won a holiday for two in the Maldives.

At the end of the round, the bingo caller went over

to him and said: 'You must be the luckiest man in the world! You have won fifteen thousand dollars, a car and a fantastic luxury holiday in just one game!'

'I'm not that lucky,' replied the man. 'I've got B55.'

The bingo caller's face turned to shock and he said: 'You lucky bastard! You've won the raffle as well!'

A man said to his friend: 'I went to the dentist this morning.'

'So does your tooth still hurt?' asked the friend.

'I don't know. He kept it.'

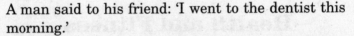

A young woman was suffering from terrible toothache but was reluctant to go to the dentist because she was scared of the drill. Eventually she was in such pain that she summoned the courage to go.

'I am absolutely terrified,' she told the dentist as she entered the surgery. 'In fact, I think I'd rather have a baby than have a tooth drilled.'

'Well,' said the dentist, 'make up your mind before I adjust the chair.'

Did you hear about the man who had a phobia of hurdles?

– Eventually he got over it.

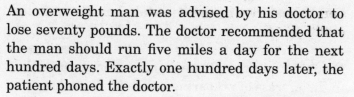

An overweight man was advised by his doctor to lose seventy pounds. The doctor recommended that the man should run five miles a day for the next hundred days. Exactly one hundred days later, the patient phoned the doctor.

'Have you lost the weight?' asked the doctor.

'Yes, I have,' said the man, 'but I'm not very happy about the situation.'

'Why not?'

'Because I'm five hundred miles from home!'

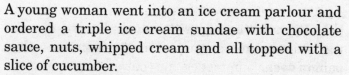

A young woman went into an ice cream parlour and ordered a triple ice cream sundae with chocolate sauce, nuts, whipped cream and all topped with a slice of cucumber.

The waiter said: 'Did I hear you correctly? Did you say you wanted it topped with a slice of cucumber?'

'Sorry,' said the woman. 'I don't know what I was thinking. Forget the cucumber. I'm on a diet.'

Laws of Dieting

If you eat something when nobody is watching, it has no calories.

When drinking a diet cola while eating a chocolate bar, the calories in the chocolate bar are cancelled out by the diet cola.

Food that is licked off knives, spoons or container lids in the process of preparing a dish has no calories.

Foods that are the same colour have the same number of calories – e.g. spinach and pistachio ice cream.

Broken cookies or chocolate bars contain no calories as the process of breaking causes the calories to fall out.

When you are eating with somebody else, calories don't count unless you eat more than the other person does.

Movie-related foods such as popcorn don't count because they are part of the entertainment package and not part of your personal fuel.

What should you do if your girlfriend starts smoking?
– Slow down and use a lubricant.

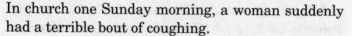

In church one Sunday morning, a woman suddenly had a terrible bout of coughing.

Afterwards a friend said to the woman's husband: 'I felt really sorry for Sylvia having that coughing fit, and the way everyone turned to look at her.'

'Don't worry,' said the husband. 'She was wearing a new hat.'

A man tried every known diet in an attempt to lose weight, but none worked. Then one day he spotted an ad in the paper that read: 'Lose weight, a dollar a pound.'

So he phoned the number in the ad, and the voice on the other end said: 'How much weight do you want to lose?'

The man answered: 'Ten pounds.'

The voice replied: 'Put your cheque in the mail, and we'll send one of our representatives over to your house first thing in the morning.'

At nine o'clock the next morning there was a knock on the door of the man's house. He opened it to find a beautiful brunette standing there naked except for a sign around her neck that said: 'If you catch me, you can screw me.'

The overweight man chased her all over the house – up the stairs, through the kitchen, over the couch and finally he caught her. After fantastic sex, the brunette said: 'Quick. Go to the bathroom and weigh yourself.' He did, and discovered that he had lost ten pounds exactly.

That evening he called the number again. The voice on the other end said: 'How much weight do you want to lose?'

The man replied: 'Twenty pounds.'

'Very well,' said the voice. 'Put your cheque in the mail and one of our representatives will be at your house first thing in the morning.'

Sure enough at eight o'clock the next morning there was a knock on the door of the man's house. He opened it to find a gorgeous blonde wearing only running shoes and with a sign around her neck saying: 'If you can catch me, you can screw me.'

Even though the man had lost weight, the blonde was extremely agile and the chase took a little longer than before, but eventually he caught her and had amazing sex with her. When he had finished, she said: 'Quick. Go to the bathroom and weigh yourself.' He did, and discovered that he had lost twenty pounds exactly.

Scarcely able to believe his luck, the man called the number again that evening. The voice on the other end said: 'How much weight do you want to lose?'

'Fifty pounds,' said the man.

'Fifty pounds?' asked the voice. 'That's a lot of weight to lose at one time!'

'Don't worry,' said the man. 'My cheque's already in the mail. You just have your representative here in the morning.' Then he hung up.

At seven o'clock the next morning there was a knock on the door of the man's house. He opened it to find a huge gorilla standing there with a sign around its neck saying: 'If I catch you, I'm going to screw you.'

Heaven and Hell

A man arrived at the gates of Heaven and St Peter asked: 'What religion are you?'

'Methodist,' replied the man.

St Peter consulted his list and said: 'Okay, Methodist. Go to room 20 but please be quiet as you pass room 6.'

Moments later, another man arrived at the gates of Heaven.

'Religion?' asked St Peter.

'Catholic,' said the man.

'Right, Catholic,' said St Peter looking at his list. 'Go to room 15 but be quiet as you pass room 6.'

Meanwhile a third man had arrived at the gates. 'What religion are you?' asked St Peter.

'Baptist,' said the man.

'Fine,' said St Peter. 'Baptists are in room 28, so go there but be quiet as you pass room 6.'

The Baptist said: 'I understand why there are different rooms for different religions but why must we be quiet when we pass room 6?'

St Peter said: 'Because the Jehovah's Witnesses are in room 6, and they think they're the only ones here.'

Sister Rosemary, a nun, went to Heaven, but was told by St Peter that there was a waiting list for entry. 'Go home and relax,' he suggested. 'Give me a call in a week and I'll let you know whether your accommodation is ready.'

The following week she phoned and said: 'Peter, this is Rosemary. I have a confession to make: I smoked my first-ever cigarette yesterday. Do you think it will affect my chances of getting into Heaven?'

'We're not that strict!' laughed St Peter. 'So I'm sure one cigarette won't spoil your chances. But I'm afraid your room still isn't ready, so give me a call in a week.'

A week later, she called again. 'Peter, this is Rosemary. I have a confession to make: I had my first-ever alcoholic drink yesterday. Do you think it will affect my chances of getting into Heaven?'

'I don't think one drink will prevent you getting into Heaven,' said St Peter. 'But I'm afraid your room still isn't ready, so give me a call in three days.'

Three days later, she rang again. 'Peter, this is Rosemary. I have a confession to make: last night I kissed a man for the first time. Do you think it will ruin my chances of getting into Heaven?'

'I shouldn't think so,' said St Peter. 'But I couldn't say for certain. Give me a ring tomorrow. By then I'll have got an answer from God and I'll know about your accommodation.'

The next day, she phoned again. 'Pete, this is Rosie. Forget about the room.'

A cat and a mouse died on the same day and went up to Heaven. On his first day there, the mouse met God who asked him: 'How do you like it in Heaven?' 'It's great,' said the mouse, 'but it's so vast that I don't think I'll ever get to see it all. It would be really nice if I had some form of transport.'

So God gave the mouse a pair of roller skates.

The next day, God saw the cat and asked him:

'How do you like it in Heaven?'

'It's great,' said the cat, just as the mouse rode past on his roller skates, 'and I didn't know you had meals on wheels up here.'

Three nuns were killed in a road accident and went to Heaven. When they arrived at the Pearly Gates, St Peter said: 'You ladies have led exemplary lives, but before I can admit you, I must ask you each one religious-based question.'

So he asked the first nun: 'What was the name of the first man that God created?'

'Adam,' replied the nun. Lights flashed, music played, angels sang and the nun was admitted to Heaven.

Then St Peter asked the second nun: 'What was the name of the first woman that God created?'

'Eve,' answered the nun. Lights flashed, music played, angels sang and the nun was admitted to Heaven.

Then St Peter asked the third nun: 'What was the first thing that Eve said to Adam?'

Baffled, the nun scratched her head and said: 'Gee, that's a hard one.'

Lights flashed, music played, angels sang . . .

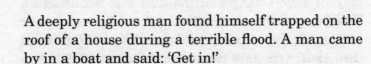

St Peter noticed a man pacing up and down outside the Pearly Gates. 'Can I help you?' asked St Peter.

The man looked impatiently at his watch. 'No, it's okay,' he replied. 'I won't be long.'

A few minutes later, St Peter looked out again and saw that the man was becoming increasingly agitated. 'What's the problem?' asked St Peter.

'Listen,' said the man. 'You know I'm dead; I know I'm dead. So will someone please tell the cardiac arrest team?'

A deeply religious man found himself trapped on the roof of a house during a terrible flood. A man came by in a boat and said: 'Get in!'

But the religious man said: 'No, I have faith in God. He will grant me a miracle.'

Soon the water was up to his waist and another man came by in a boat and shouted: 'Get in!'

But the religious man said: 'No, I have faith in God. He will grant me a miracle.'

With the water up to his chest, a third boat passed by. 'Get in!' shouted the boatman.

But the religious man replied: 'No, I have faith in

God. He will grant me a miracle.'

With the water up to his chin, a helicopter threw down a ladder and the crew told him to climb up.

But the religious man spluttered: 'No, I still have faith in God. He will grant me a miracle.'

Half an hour later, he arrived at the Gates of Heaven, his faith broken. He told St Peter: 'I feel I have been let down. I really was convinced that God would grant me a miracle.'

'Be fair,' said St Peter. 'We did send you three boats and a helicopter.'

Three men – Jeff, Phil and Mike – found themselves in Hell. No sooner had they arrived than a door in a wall opened and they saw a really ugly woman, her face covered in warts. The voice of the Devil boomed out: 'Jeff, you have sinned. You are condemned to spend the rest of eternity in bed with this poor woman.' And Jeff was led through the door to suffer his punishment.

The other two men were understandably wary when a second door opened to reveal a woman even uglier than the first. She had one eye, no teeth, a hunched back and she stank of manure. Her body was covered in flies. The voice of the Devil boomed out: 'Phil, you have sinned. You are condemned to spend the rest of eternity in bed with this wretched woman.' And Phil was led through the door to suffer his punishment.

By now Mike was a nervous wreck. So he feared the worst when a third door opened, but to his enormous relief he saw a beautiful blonde standing there wearing a skimpy bikini. 'Wow!' he thought. Then he heard the voice of the Devil boom out: 'Carla, you have sinned. . .'

Three men died and went to Heaven. At the Pearly Gates, St Peter told them: 'Heaven is a big place, so you're going to need transport to get around. We will determine what type of vehicle you get according to how faithful you were to your wives.'

Turning to the first man, St Peter said: 'How faithful were you to your wife?'

The first man replied: 'I never once strayed. From the day I first met her to the day I died, she was the only woman I slept with. I loved her very much.'

'As a reward for your fidelity,' said St Peter, 'I present you with the keys to a magnificent Rolls-Royce.'

Then St Peter addressed the second man and asked him if he was faithful to his wife. 'Well,' said the second man hesitantly, 'I must admit I did have the odd fling in my youth, but I did love my wife and after those lapses I remained faithful to her until my dying day.'

'Very well,' said St Peter, 'as a reward for your good behaviour I award the keys to a Pontiac.'

Finally St Peter asked the third man: 'Were you faithful to your wife?'

The third man hung his head in shame. 'I regret to say I slept with everyone and anyone. I played the field throughout our marriage. I had dozens of affairs, some lasting for over a year, as well as countless one-night stands. Nevertheless I still loved my wife and always went back to her.'

'Your behaviour left a lot to be desired,' said St Peter, 'but you say you did love your wife, so that does count for something. Therefore I will give you a ten-speed bicycle.'

The three men spent the next two weeks travelling around Heaven in their respective vehicles. Then one day, the man on the bicycle saw the man with the Rolls-Royce sobbing uncontrollably by the side of the road.

'What's the matter?' he asked. 'What could possibly be wrong? You have a beautiful Rolls-Royce to drive around in.'

'I know,' said the man with the Rolls-Royce between sobs, 'but I've just seen my wife go past on a skateboard.'

Law and Order

A police officer spotted a man driving erratically. Pulling him over, the officer asked: 'Have you been drinking?'

'Yes, I have,' replied the man. 'I started out with a couple of pints at the Coach and Horses, then I had a couple more at that new bar on Church Street, then I moved on to the Red Lion where I had four or five vodkas and then I bought a bottle of whisky, which I've just finished.'

'Right,' said the officer, 'I need you to step out of the car and take a breathalyser test.'

'What's the matter?' asked the man. 'Don't you believe me?'

A burglar broke into Sting's house, but while making his escape he ran into the singer himself in the street.

'Hey, Sting,' he called out. 'I've got all your records!'

A man appeared in court on a double murder charge. The judge said: 'You are charged with beating your wife to death with a spanner.'

Hearing this, a man in the public gallery shouted: 'You bastard!'

The judge went on: 'You are also charged with beating your wife's lover to death with a spanner.'

Again the man in the public gallery yelled out: 'You bastard!'

The judge turned to the public gallery and said: 'Sir, I can understand your outrage at this terrible crime, but I will not tolerate any more outbursts.'

'I'm sorry, Your Honour,' said the man, 'but for twelve years I lived next door to that bastard – and every time I asked to borrow a spanner, he told me he didn't have one!'

Police arrested two children. One was drinking battery acid, the other was eating fireworks. They charged one and let the other one off.

A man spotted burglars breaking into his garden shed one night, so he phoned the police, but they said there were no available cars in his area.

He hung up, waited a minute and then phoned the police again. 'I rang just now about the burglars in my garden shed. Well, there's no need to worry because I've just shot them.'

Within minutes, three patrol cars screeched to a halt outside his house – just in time to arrest the burglars.

One of the officers marched over to the householder and said: 'I thought you said you'd shot them!'

The man replied: 'And I thought you said there were no cars available!'

The defendant stood defiantly in the dock and said to the judge: 'I don't recognize this court.'

'Why?' barked the judge.

'Because you've had it decorated since the last time I was here.'

Three men attended a job interview to join the FBI. The first man walked into the office, and the FBI agent who was conducting the interviews explained: 'To be in the FBI, you must be loyal, dedicated and willing to obey orders. Here's the scenario: your wife is sitting on a chair in the next room, and I want you go in there and shoot her with this gun.'

The man took the gun, but then hesitated and said: 'Sorry, I can't do it.'

Next it was the second man's turn to be interviewed. The FBI agent told him: 'To be in the FBI, you must be loyal, dedicated and willing to obey orders. Here's the scenario: your wife is sitting on a chair in the next room, and I want you to go in there and shoot her with this gun.'

The man took the gun, walked into the room, but then immediately walked out again. 'Sorry,' he said, 'I can't do it.'

Finally it was the third man's turn. The FBI agent said: 'To be in the FBI, you must be loyal, dedicated and willing to obey orders. Here's the scenario: your wife is sitting on a chair in the next room, and I want you to go in there and shoot her with this gun.'

The man took the gun and went into the room.

The agent heard six shots, silence, then a lot of screaming.

Seconds later, the man came out of the room, saying: 'Some idiot loaded the gun with blanks, so I had to beat her to death with the chair!'

A rookie cop was on his first day in a patrol car, where he was teamed up with a more experienced partner. Nothing much happened for the first hour but then a call came through asking them to disperse a group of people who were loitering on the corner of Main Street.

'I'll deal with this,' said the rookie excitedly. So when they reached Main Street and saw a small crowd on the corner, he jumped out of the car and yelled: 'Okay, move along now. Quick as you can. Haven't you got homes to go to?'

The crowd were reluctant to disperse so he repeated the command more forcefully: 'Come on now, move on or I'll start taking names and addresses.'

Puzzled, they slowly drifted off in different directions and the rookie returned to the patrol car.

'Not bad, huh?' he said proudly to his partner.

'Yeah, you did okay. Pity it was a bus stop . . .'

The defendant's barrister said: 'Madam, could you please explain to this court how you came to stab your husband ninety-three times?'

'Yes,' she replied. 'I couldn't turn off the electric knife.'

A hardened inmate at a tough, maximum-security jail said to a new young prisoner: 'I've got two tickets for the warden's ball. Do you want to buy one?'

'No thanks,' replied the newcomer. 'I can't dance.'

'It's not a dance, it's a raffle!'

Signs That Your Police Partner Needs a Vacation

Every Wednesday, he insists it's his turn to be the siren.

He keeps asking if his bulletproof vest makes him look fat.

He talks to himself. Half of him is the 'good cop', the other half is the 'bad cop'.

He wants to play Scrabble with his colleagues instead of poker.

He keeps handcuffing himself by accident.

He won't enter a building alone at night because he's afraid the bogeyman will get him.

He wants to hear less talk and more music on the police channel.

He starts exchanging doughnut recipes with complete strangers.

He wants to add a nice lace trim to his uniform.

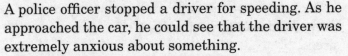

A police officer stopped a driver for speeding. As he approached the car, he could see that the driver was extremely anxious about something.

'Good afternoon, sir,' said the officer. 'Do you know why I stopped you?'

'Yes, officer,' replied the driver. 'I know I was speeding. But it is a matter of life and death.'

'In what way?'

'There's a naked woman waiting for me at home.'

'I don't see how that is a matter of life and death.'

'Oh yes it is. If I don't get home before my wife does, I'm a dead man!'

A police officer arrested a man and told him: 'I'm afraid I'm going to have to lock you up for the night.'

'What's the charge?' asked the suspect.

'Oh, there's no charge,' said the officer. 'It's all part of the service.'

Halfway through a lengthy cross-examination of a witness, a barrister stopped and said: 'I object, Your Honour! One of the jurors is asleep!'

The judge replied curtly: 'You put him to sleep. . . you wake him up!'

A man in a hurry taking his eight-year-old son to school made a right turn at a red light.

'Uh-oh!' he said. 'I think I just made an illegal turn.'

'It's okay, Dad,' said the boy. 'The police car right behind us did the same thing.'

Two new prisoners were led to their cell. 'How long are you in for?' asked one.

'Eighteen years. What about you?'

'Twenty-five years. So as you're getting out first, you'd better have the bed by the door.'

A man in a ski mask ran into a bank, pointed a banana at the cashier and yelled: 'This is a cock-up!'

'Don't you mean a stick-up?' asked the cashier.

'No,' said the robber. 'It's a cock-up. I forgot to bring the gun!'

A traffic cop pulled over a driver who had been weaving erratically along the highway. Approaching the car, he said: 'Sir, I need you to blow into this breathalyser.'

'Sorry, officer,' he replied. 'I can't do that. I'm an asthmatic. If I do that, I'll have a really bad asthma attack.'

'Well, then I need you to come down to the station to give me a blood sample.'

'I can't do that either, officer. I'm a haemophiliac. If I do that, I'll bleed to death.'

'Well perhaps we could try a urine sample?'

'Sorry, officer, I can't do that either. I'm also a diabetic. If I do that, I'll get really low blood sugar.'

'Okay then,' said the officer, growing increasingly exasperated, 'I need you to step out of the car and walk along that white line.'

'I can't do that, officer.'

'Why the hell not?'

'Because I'm drunk.'

A lawyer walked into his client's cell on death row and said: 'I've got good news and bad news.'

'What's the bad news?' asked the client.

'The bad news is that the state governor has refused your plea for a stay of execution.'

'Oh, my God! So I'm gonna die. What could possibly be the good news?'

The lawyer said: 'I've managed to get your voltage reduced.'

A shipment of Viagra was hijacked last week. Police officers are on the lookout for a gang of hardened criminals.

A man with a scarf covering the lower half of his face burst into a bank brandishing a sawn-off shotgun but as he grabbed the money his mask slipped. He quickly pulled it back up again but panicked that someone might have seen his face.

Pointing the gun at a couple standing nearby, he growled at the man: 'Did you see my face, because if you did I'll have to kill you?'

'No, I didn't see your face,' said the man.

'Are you sure?' yelled the robber.

'Absolutely,' replied the man, 'but I'm fairly certain my wife did.'

A police officer stopped a driver who was speeding down Main Street.

'But officer,' the man said. 'I can explain . . .'

'Keep quiet and save it for later,' said the officer. 'I'm going to let you cool your heels in jail until the chief gets back.'

'But officer, I just wanted to say . . .'

'And I said, "Keep quiet!" You're going to jail.'

An hour and a half later, the officer looked in on his prisoner and said: 'Lucky for you that the chief's at his daughter's wedding. He'll be in a good mood when he gets back.'

'Don't count on it,' said the prisoner. 'I'm the groom!'

How many police officers does it take to break an egg?
– None. It fell down the stairs.

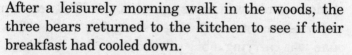

After a leisurely morning walk in the woods, the three bears returned to the kitchen to see if their breakfast had cooled down.

'Someone's eaten my porridge!' cried baby bear.

'And someone's eaten my porridge!' wailed mother bear.

'Never mind the porridge!' said father bear. 'Where's the flat screen TV?'

The judge looked at the defendant and asked: 'What exactly is it you're charged with?'

'Doing my Christmas shopping early,' replied the defendant.

'That's not an offence,' said the judge. 'How early were you doing this shopping?'

The defendant bowed his head and said: 'Before the store opened.'

Following the theft of a truck full of toupees, police officers were reported to be combing the area.

A man on a bicycle was stopped at the US border by police officers investigating a smuggling racket. The man was carrying a bag of sand, but after searching the bag the police found nothing untoward and let him go.

The next week, the same man on a bicycle was again stopped at the border carrying a bag of sand. Again the officers searched the bag thoroughly but found nothing illegal and sent him on his way.

This went on for three years. Then one day the police officers bumped into the man in a bar. 'Listen,' they said, 'we know you're up to something, but our curiosity's killing us. If we promise not to prosecute you, will you tell us what it is you've been smuggling across the border for the last three years?'

The man smiled and answered: 'Bicycles.'

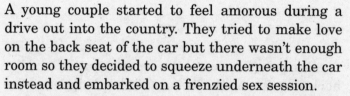

A young couple started to feel amorous during a drive out into the country. They tried to make love on the back seat of the car but there wasn't enough room so they decided to squeeze underneath the car instead and embarked on a frenzied sex session.

Some ten minutes later, a police officer appeared on the scene and informed them that he was arresting them for indecent exposure.

'But all I'm doing under here is repairing the car,' protested the young man.

'You're having sex,' said the officer. 'And there are three reasons why I know that. Firstly, you have no tools out. Secondly, I can see two pairs of legs. And thirdly, your car's been stolen.'

Five thousand bars of soap were stolen from a warehouse. Police say the thieves made a clean getaway.

Two men had just broken into a high-rise apartment when they heard the sound of police sirens.

'Quick! Let's jump out the window.'

'We can't,' said his accomplice. 'We're on the thirteenth floor.'

'Listen, this is no time to be superstitious.'

A police patrol car was keeping observation on a bar at closing time on the lookout for drunk drivers. Sure enough, the two officers watched a man stumble out of the bar, trip over the kerb and fumble for his car keys for several minutes. When he eventually managed to get into the car, it took him another five minutes to get the key in the ignition. Meanwhile all the other customers had left the bar and driven off. When the man finally set the car in motion, the officers seized their chance, pulling him over and ordering him to do a breathalyser test.

To their amazement, the test showed no trace of alcohol. So they made him breathe into the bag again, but the result was the same.

'That can't be right,' said one of the officers.

'Yes, it can,' said the man. 'Tonight I'm the designated decoy.'

Why did the escaped convict saw the legs off his bed?
– He wanted to lie low.

Cross-examining a witness, an arrogant defence barrister asked pointedly: 'But did you actually see the accused bite off Mr Brown's ear?

'No,' replied the witness. 'But I did see him spit it out.'

Lawyers

A man was walking through a park when he spotted an old bottle. He rubbed it and a genie appeared.

'I will grant you three wishes,' said the genie, 'but I must warn you that for each of your wishes every lawyer in the world will receive double what you ask for.'

'I understand,' said the man. 'My first wish is for a Rolls-Royce.'

POOF! A Rolls-Royce appeared in front of him, and the genie said: 'Now every lawyer in the world has been given two Rolls-Royces. What is your next wish?'

'My second wish', said the man, 'is for a million dollars.'

POOF! A million dollars appeared in front of him, and the genie said: 'Now every lawyer in the world has been given two million dollars. What is your final wish?'

The man thought for a moment and said: 'Well, I've always wanted to donate a kidney . . .'

What's the difference between a good lawyer and a bad lawyer?
– A bad lawyer can let a case drag on for several years. A good lawyer can make it last even longer.

A lawyer died and was standing in front of St Peter at the Pearly Gates. St Peter said: 'You're a lawyer, you can't come in here – you have to go to the other place.'

But using all his courtroom know-how, the lawyer pleaded his case until St Peter reconsidered. 'Okay, this is what I'll do,' said St Peter. 'You will spend the same amount of time in Hell as you did on Earth, and then you can spend the rest of eternity up here.'

'Fair enough,' said the lawyer.

'So,' said St Peter, 'we'll see you in three hundred and eighty-five years.'

'What do you mean three hundred and eighty-five years?' said the lawyer. 'I'm only fifty-nine.'

'I know,' said St Peter, 'but we go by billing hours.'

The glass tanks were accidentally left open in the zoo's reptile house, as a result of which all of the snakes escaped. With highly venomous reptiles on the loose, the head keeper desperately tried to round them up, but to no avail.

Eventually he turned to his assistant and said: 'It's no use. We'll have to call a lawyer.'

'A lawyer?' said the assistant. 'Why will a lawyer be of any use?'

'Because', said the head keeper, 'we need someone who speaks their language.'

A young lawyer was involved in a horrific car smash. The entire side of his Ferrari was ripped away, along with his arm. When a police officer arrived on the scene, the lawyer was in a state of shock. 'My car! My car!' he wailed.

Seeing how badly the lawyer was injured, the officer said: 'Sir, I think you ought to be more worried about your arm than your car.'

The lawyer looked down in horror at where his arm used to be and screamed: 'My Rolex! My Rolex!'

A lawyer who had been drinking was driving home when he rear-ended the car in front. He got out of his car, walked over to the driver of the other car and sneered: 'Boy, are you in trouble! I'm a lawyer.'

The other driver looked out of his window and said: 'No, you're in trouble. I'm a judge!'

How many lawyers does it take to roof a house?
– It depends on how thin you slice them.

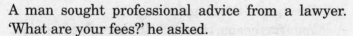

A man sought professional advice from a lawyer. 'What are your fees?' he asked.

'Seventy-five dollars for three questions,' replied the lawyer.

'That's pretty expensive, isn't it?'

'Maybe,' said the lawyer. 'So, what's your third question?'

What's the difference between a lawyer and a herd of buffalo?

– A lawyer charges more.

A truck driver detested lawyers with a vengeance. In fact if he ever saw any lawyers walking by the side of the road he would deliberately swerve his truck into them and run them down. He loved the THUD sound as the truck hit the lawyers.

One day, the truck driver saw a priest hitchhiking by the side of the road. 'Where are you going to, Father?' he asked.

'St Michael's church, about five miles down the road,' replied the priest.

'Climb in,' said the truck driver, and he set off in the direction of the church.

A mile further on, the truck driver spotted a lawyer walking by the side of the road and instinctively swerved to hit him. But at the last minute he remembered he had a priest as a passenger and so he veered back into the middle of the road, narrowly avoiding the lawyer. However he still heard the THUD sound. Puzzled, he turned to the priest and said: 'I'm sorry, Father. I nearly hit that lawyer.'

'Don't worry,' said the priest. 'I got him with the door!'

Marriage and Divorce

A husband arrived home from work to find his wife in bed with his friend. Angered by the betrayal, the husband rushed into the study, produced a gun and shot him dead.

His wife shook her head in despair and said: 'If you keep behaving like this, you'll lose all of your friends.'

A man went into a florist's and asked for a very big bunch of flowers.

'How big exactly?' asked the florist.

The man replied: 'Caught in bed with my sister-in-law size.'

What's the difference between a heavily pregnant woman and a supermodel?
– Nothing, if the husband knows what's good for him.

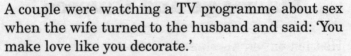

A couple were watching a TV programme about sex when the wife turned to the husband and said: 'You make love like you decorate.'

'What, you mean very slow and professional?'

'No,' she replied curtly. 'Fast and sloppy and I have to finish the job myself.'

A travelling salesman was testifying in divorce proceedings against his wife. His attorney said: 'Please describe the incident which first led you to suspect that your wife was being unfaithful.'

The salesman answered: 'I'm on the road during the week, so naturally when I get home at weekends I am particularly attentive to my wife. One Sunday morning we were in the middle of a passionate sex session when the old lady in the apartment next door banged on the wall and yelled: 'Can't you at least stop that racket at the weekend?'

A married man was having an affair with his secretary. One afternoon, they went to her house and made passionate love, after which they fell asleep. When they awoke, it was eight o'clock in the evening. He hurriedly threw on his clothes, and told his lover to take his shoes outside and rub them on the grass and dirt. Mystified, she did as he asked. He then put on his shoes and drove home.

'Where the hell have you been?' his wife demanded as he entered the house.

'I can't lie to you, honey,' he replied. 'I'm having an affair with my secretary and we've been having sex all afternoon. I fell asleep and didn't wake up until eight o'clock.'

His wife glanced down at his shoes and yelled: 'You lying bastard! You've been playing golf!'

A man and his wife were giving each other the silent treatment. After ten days of this, he realized that he needed her to wake him the following morning so that he could catch the 8 a.m. flight to Los Angeles for an important business meeting. Not wanting to be the first to break the silence, he wrote on a piece of paper: 'Please wake me at 5 a.m.'

The next morning, he woke up, only to find that it was 9 a.m. He'd missed his flight. Furious, he was about to ask his wife why she hadn't woken him when he noticed a piece of paper next to the bed. It read: 'It's 5 a.m. Wake up.'

A young couple met with the minister to set a date for their wedding. When the minister asked whether they would prefer a modern or a traditional service, they chose the modern service.

On the day of the wedding, there was a terrible storm that forced the groom to abandon the car and complete his journey to the church on foot. The roads were flooded, so he rolled up his trousers in a bid to keep them dry. Arriving late at church, he was immediately hustled up the aisle so that the ceremony could start.

The minister took one look at him and hissed: 'Pull down your trousers.'

Alarmed by this, the groom said: 'Uh, actually, minister, I've changed my mind. I think I'll go for the traditional service.'

A man asked his wife what she wanted for her birthday. 'Well,' she said optimistically, eyeing his new Chevrolet parked on the drive, 'a little something to run around in would be nice.'

So he bought her a tracksuit.

Friends Jo and Kelly both had marriages that were going through rocky patches. One day Jo said: 'I'm going to get a divorce. Yesterday I saw my creep of a husband going into a movie with another woman.'

'There could have been an innocent explanation,' said Kelly, trying to reassure her. 'Why didn't you follow them into the cinema?'

'I couldn't,' said Jo. 'The guy I was with had already seen the movie.'

A man and his wife went out for a drink one evening. After a few drinks, he suddenly said: 'I love you.'

Unaccustomed to such displays of affection, she said: 'Is that you or the beer talking?'

He answered: 'It's me – I'm talking to the beer.'

A man confided to his friend: 'Something terrible has happened. I was away on business, and I emailed my wife to tell her that I'd be back a day early. I rushed home from the airport and found her in bed with our next-door neighbour. How could she do that to me?'

'Don't be too hard on her,' said the friend. 'Maybe she didn't read your email.'

A young couple were preparing to get married, but as the wedding day approached they became increasingly nervous. For each had a problem they had never shared with anyone, not even each other.

Finally overcoming his embarrassment, the groom decided to confide in his father. 'Dad,' he said, 'I'm really worried about this marriage.'

'Why?' asked his father. 'Are you having second thoughts?'

'I do love her,' replied the son, 'but I'm not sure how she'll cope with my feet. In case you hadn't noticed, they're always horribly smelly and I'm afraid they'll put her off.'

'No problem,' said the father. 'All you have to do is wash your feet as often as possible, and always wear socks, even to bed.'

The son thanked him for his advice, and promised to follow it.

Meanwhile the bride-to-be had finally plucked up the courage to confide in her mother. 'Mum,' she said, 'when I wake up in the morning, my breath is truly awful.'

'But honey,' said her mother comfortingly, 'everyone has bad breath in the morning.'

'No, you don't understand,' said the daughter. 'My breath in the morning is so horrendously rancid that I'm afraid my husband won't want to sleep in the same room as me.'

Her mother considered the problem for a moment and then said: 'There is a solution. Every morning, as soon as you wake up you must get out of bed and go straight to the kitchen to make breakfast. While your husband is busy eating, slip into the bathroom and brush your teeth. The important thing is not to say a word until you have brushed your teeth.'

'I shouldn't even say good morning?' queried the daughter.

'No, not a word,' the mother insisted.

So the daughter promised to give it a try.

Two weeks later, the couple were married and, remembering the advice each had received – he with his perpetual socks and she with her morning silence – they managed quite well.

But then four months into their married life, the husband woke just before dawn one morning to find that one of his socks had come off. Fearful of the consequences, he frantically searched the bed, and in doing so woke his wife.

Without thinking, she asked: 'What are you doing?'

'Oh my God!' he replied in horror, recoiling from her breath. 'You've swallowed my sock!'

A man confided to his friend: 'I haven't spoken to my wife for five months.'

'Why not?' asked the friend.

'I don't like to interrupt her.'

A man bought his forty-four-year-old wife a new line of expensive cosmetics guaranteed to make her look years younger. After carefully applying them, she said: 'Darling, tell me honestly. What age do you think I look?'

Studying her closely, he replied: 'From your skin, twenty-one; your hair, eighteen; and your figure, twenty-five.'

'Oh, you do flatter me!' she grinned.

'Hang on,' he said. 'I haven't added them up yet!'

Bill ran into an old school friend Tom at the supermarket. 'I hear you got married again, Tom,' he said.

'Yes,' said Tom, 'for the fourth time!'

'Wow! What happened to your first three wives?'

'They all died.'

'I'm sorry, I didn't know. That's terrible. How did they die?'

'The first ate poisonous mushrooms.'

'How awful! What about the second?'

'She ate poisonous mushrooms.'

'Oh no! What about the third? Did she die from eating poisonous mushrooms, too?'

'No, she died of a broken neck.'

'Oh right, an accident?'

'Not exactly – you see, she wouldn't eat her mushrooms.'

A man married a woman who had an identical twin but within a year he was filing for divorce.

'Tell the court why you want a divorce,' said the judge.

'Well, Your Honour,' explained the man, 'every once in a while my sister-in-law would come over for a visit and because she and my wife looked exactly alike, now and then I'd end up making love to her by mistake.'

'Surely there must be some difference between the two women?' said the judge.

'You'd better believe it!' replied the man. 'That's why I want the divorce!'

Did you hear about the couple who met in a revolving door?
– They're still going round together.

While out on a hot date one night, a man parked his car in a quiet street and climbed into the back seat for sex. His partner was insatiable, and after two hours of passionate lovemaking she still wanted more. The man, however, was exhausted.

Eventually he said: 'Excuse me, but I must go for a pee.'

He climbed out of the car and noticed a man further down the street struggling to change a tyre. He went over to him and said: 'Listen, I've got this woman in my car who's driving me crazy for sex. We've done it four times but she still wants more. I don't think I can manage it again. So if I change your tyre, will you take my place?'

The second man agreed and climbed into the back

seat with the willing woman. They were just getting started when a passing police officer tapped on the car window and shone a torch on them.

'What are you doing in there?' asked the officer.

'I'm making love to my wife,' replied the man hesitantly.

'Well, this is a public place,' said the officer. 'Can't you do that at home?'

'Actually, officer,' said the man, 'I didn't know it was my wife until you shone the torch on her!'

Marriage . . . Divorce

She married him because he was such a 'strong man'.
She divorced him because he was such a 'domineering male'.

He married her because she was so 'fragile and petite'.
He divorced her because she was so 'weak and helpless'.

She married him because 'he knows how to provide a good living'.
She divorced him because 'all he thinks about is business'.

He married her because she was 'steady and sensible'.
He divorced her because she was 'boring and dull'.

She married him because he was 'a hit with women'.
She divorced him because he was 'a hit with other women'.

He married her because 'she reminds me of my mother'.
He divorced her because 'she gets more like her mother every day'.

A mother was anxiously awaiting her teenage daughter's return home from a year backpacking abroad. As the passengers came through the door into the airport arrivals lounge, the mother noticed that right behind her daughter was a man dressed in feathers with exotic markings all over his body, and carrying a shrunken head. Seeing her mother, the daughter ran up to her, flung her arms around her and then introduced the strange-looking man as her new husband.

The mother threw up her hands in horror. 'You never listen to me, darling!' she screamed. 'You never listen! I said for you to marry a RICH doctor. A RICH doctor!'

A woman screamed at her husband: 'You're gonna be real sorry. I'm gonna leave you!'

'Make up your mind,' said the husband. 'Which is it gonna be?'

A man told his priest that he was thinking about getting a divorce. 'Why would you want to divorce such a lovely woman as Linda?' asked the priest. 'She is soft and gentle and, if I may say so, quite beautiful and nicely proportioned. I can't think what more you could wish for from a wife.'

The man took off his shoe. 'See this shoe,' he said, showing it to the priest. 'The leather is soft and gentle. It is a quite beautiful piece of craftsmanship and nicely proportioned . . . but only I know how it pinches.'

'It's too hot to wear clothes today,' said the husband stepping out of the shower. 'What do you reckon the neighbours will think if I mow the grass like this?'

'Probably that I married you for your money,' answered his wife.

Shopping at a supermarket, a married man noticed a pretty young woman waving at him and mouthing 'hello'. But he was puzzled because he couldn't place her. So when he caught up with her, said: 'I'm sorry. Do you know me?'

'I think you're the father of one of my kids,' she replied.

He started to panic. His mind raced back to the only time he had ever been unfaithful to his wife and he blurted out: 'My God, are you the stripper from the office Christmas party who got me so worked up we had sex right there and then on the desk while all my colleagues sprayed whipped cream on us?'

'No,' she replied calmly. 'Actually I'm your son's maths teacher.'

A girl brought home her fiancé, a theology student, to meet her parents for the first time. Her father was keen to learn what prospects the boy had.

'How do you intend to make a living?' asked the father.

'I don't know,' said the student, 'but God will provide.'

The father raised his eyebrows. 'Do you own a car?'

'No,' replied the student, 'but God will provide.'

'I see. And where are you thinking of living once you're married?'

'No idea, but I am sure God will provide.'

Later the mother asked the father what he thought of their prospective son-in-law.

'Not a lot really,' sighed the father. 'He's got no money and seems to have given precious little thought to the future. But on the other hand he thinks I'm God!'

A young man paid a first visit to his wife's family for Sunday lunch. As he sat down at the table, his mother-in-law asked him: 'How many potatoes would you like?'

'Just one,' he replied.

'It's okay,' she said, 'there's no need to be polite.'

'Very well,' he said. 'I'll have one, you ugly old bat!'

Money

An anxious father told his son's school principal: 'I want you to stop my son gambling. All he ever seems to want to do is bet. He'll bet on anything!'

'I'll see what I can do,' said the principal.

A week later, the principal phoned the father and said: 'I think I've cured his gambling habit.'

'How have you managed that?' asked the father.

'Well,' explained the principal, 'I saw him looking at my beard and eventually he said, "I bet that's a false beard." So I asked him: "How much do you want to bet on it?" And he said, "Ten dollars."'

'What happened then?' asked the father.

'Well, he tugged my beard, which is perfectly real,

and I made him give me the ten dollars. I'm sure that's taught him a lesson and he won't be gambling anymore.'

'I wouldn't be so sure,' said the father. 'He bet me twenty dollars this morning that he'd pull your beard with your permission by the end of the week!'

A shipping magnate suddenly decided to carry out an inspection of his business. Visiting the docks unannounced, he noticed a young man leaning idly against a wall.

Disgusted by such inactivity, the magnate walked over to him and said: 'How much do you make in a day, son?'

'A hundred and twenty dollars,' replied the young man.

The magnate pulled out his wallet, gave him a hundred and twenty dollars and said: 'I've got no room for slackers in my organization. Take this money, get out of my sight and don't ever come back!'

A few minutes later the shipping clerk came over to the magnate and asked: 'Have you seen that young UPS driver? I asked him to wait here for me.'

What's the best way to stop water coming into your house?
– Don't pay the water bill.

Clive went round to his friend's house one evening and rang the doorbell. 'Is David in?' he asked.

'No,' said David's wife Carolyn, dressed in a bathrobe, 'but he should be home soon if you'd like to wait.'

So Clive sat down in the lounge with Carolyn and waited. He could hardly take his eyes off her fantastic figure. After a few minutes, he could remain silent no longer. 'Carolyn,' he said, 'I've always thought you had the most amazing breasts. If I paid you a hundred dollars, would you let me see one?'

Carolyn was surprised by the confession but secretly flattered. Anyway for that amount of money, she thought it was worth it. So she opened her robe and allowed Clive to see one of her breasts.

Clive handed over the hundred dollars and then said: 'I'd give you another hundred if I could see the other one.'

So Carolyn undid her robe a little more and this time let him have a really long look for his money. Then he gave her the hundred dollars and said: 'I'm sorry, I'm really going to have to leave. I can't wait for David any longer. Tell him I called.'

When David arrived home, Carolyn said: 'Your friend Clive came round earlier.'

'Oh, yes?' said David. 'Did he drop off the two hundred dollars he owes me?'

A man was sitting at a bar looking really miserable.

'What's up, buddy?' said the guy on the next stool. 'Do you want to talk about it?'

'I don't know,' sighed the first man. 'It's just that this time last year I had a fantastic job. I was making big money.'

'So what went wrong?'

'Well, that was the problem. People started noticing the bills were two inches too big!'

A man told his neighbour: 'A thief has stolen my wife's credit card. Last month he ran up a bill of over a thousand dollars.'

'That's awful,' said the neighbour. 'Have you reported it to the police?'

'Certainly not,' said the husband. 'He's spending less than my wife does!'

A man complained to his friend: 'My wife is always asking me for more money. A month ago she asked me for three hundred dollars, last week she said she needed two hundred dollars and yesterday she wanted a hundred dollars.'

'What does she do with it all?' asked the friend.

'I don't know,' said the husband. 'I never give her any.'

Buying car insurance, a man was surprised to be quoted a very low premium for 'fire and theft'. When he asked why it was so cheap, the insurance agent replied: 'Who'd want to steal a burnt car?'

On his first day working for a finance company, a young man was sent to try and strike a settlement with the firm's toughest client. To the amazement of his boss, he returned with the outstanding fifty-thousand-dollar debt paid in full.

'How did you get him to pay up?' asked the boss. 'We've been trying to get him to settle for over a year.'

'It was easy,' said the young man. 'I simply told him that if he didn't pay us, I'd tell all his other creditors that he had!'

A man went into a bank and asked to borrow three thousand dollars for a month. The loan officer asked what collateral the man had.

He replied: 'I've got a Rolls-Royce. Keep it until the loan is paid off. Here are the keys.'

The loan officer arranged for the vehicle to be driven into the bank's underground car park for safekeeping and gave the man the fifteen hundred dollars.

A month later, the man returned to the bank, repaid the fifteen-hundred-dollar loan plus ten dollars interest and retook possession of his Rolls-Royce.

The loan officer was puzzled. 'There's one thing I don't understand, sir,' he said. 'Why would someone who drives a Rolls-Royce need to borrow fifteen hundred dollars?'

The man replied: 'I had to go abroad for a month and where else could I store a Rolls-Royce for that length of time for ten dollars?'

A frog wanted to buy a new lily pond but had run out of money. So he went to the bank for a loan. He sat down at a desk and introduced himself as Kermit Jagger, son of Mick Jagger. He was interviewed by a bank official named Patty Whack who asked the frog what he could offer by way of collateral. The frog reached into his briefcase and pulled out a vase but Patty was not impressed.

'I'm sorry, but we'll need something more valuable than that,' she told the frog. 'It's just a cheap knick-knack.'

But just to cover her back, she decided to show the vase to the bank manager who professed to know a little about antiques. She told him: 'I've got this frog named Kermit Jagger who wants to borrow some money, and he's brought this vase in as collateral. What do you think?'

The manager registered the significance of the name, took one look at the vase and said: 'It's a knick-knack, Patty Whack, but give the frog a loan. His old man's a Rolling Stone.'

Music

Bob was sitting at the bar with a few regular customers when the bartender said: 'Go on, Bob, tell them the Elvis Presley knock-knock joke.'

'What's the Elvis Presley knock-knock joke?' asked one of the regulars.

Bob said: 'Knock knock.'

'Who's there?'

'Wurlitzer.'

'Wurlitzer who?'

'Wurlitzer one for the money, two for the show. . .'

What's the difference between a cello and a chainsaw?
– The grip.

What's the difference between a cello and a viola?
– A cello takes longer to burn.

How can you tell if a cello is out of tune?
– The bow is moving.

How do you get two viola players to play in unison?
– You shoot one of them.

What do a lawsuit and a viola have in common?
– Everyone is happier when the case is closed.

A viola player arrived home to find that his house had burnt down. A police officer informed him that the orchestra conductor had gone to the viola player's house, brutally slaughtered his family and then set fire to the building.

'What?' said the viola player, gobsmacked. 'You say the conductor actually came to my house . . . ?'

Why are harps like elderly parents?
– They're both unforgiving and difficult to get in and out of cars.

What do you get if you cross a grizzly bear and a harp?
– A bear-faced lyre.

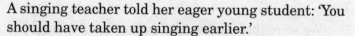

A singing teacher told her eager young student: 'You should have taken up singing earlier.'

'Why? Do you think the practice would have helped me become a star?'

'No,' said the teacher, 'but you might have given up by now.'

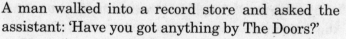

A man walked into a record store and asked the assistant: 'Have you got anything by The Doors?'

'Yes,' she said, 'a bucket and a fire extinguisher.'

What is 50 Cent known as in Zimbabwe?
– Eighty million dollars.

A girl took her boyfriend back to her house and said: 'Mum, is it okay if we go up to my room?'

'Sure, 'said the mother. 'You kids have fun.'

Shortly afterwards, the mother heard: 'Baby, baby, baby, oh!'

She rushed upstairs, opened the door to her daughter's room and yelled: 'What the hell's going on?'

'We were just having sex,' explained the daughter.

'Thank God!' said the mother. 'I thought for a minute you were listening to Justin Bieber!'

A man sitting in a bar asked the bartender: 'How late does the band play?'

The bartender replied: 'About a half-beat behind the drummer.'

What's the definition of a gentleman?
– Someone who knows how to play the bagpipes, but doesn't.

A young boy thanked his grandfather for the set of drums he bought him for his birthday. 'They're the best present I've ever had,' he said. 'They've already earned me ninety dollars.'

'That's amazing,' said the grandfather. 'You must have learned to play them real good!'

'Not really,' said the boy. 'But Mum gives me five dollars not to play them during the day, and Dad gives me five dollars not to play them in the evening.'

What do you call a beautiful girl on a trombonist's arm?
– A tattoo.

How do you get a trombonist off your porch?
– Pay for the pizza.

What's the definition of an optimist?
– A trombonist with a pager.

What type of calendar does a trombonist use for his gigs?
– Year-at-a-glance.

An intrepid explorer went in search of a remote jungle tribe with a fearsome reputation. He hired a local guide to act as translator.

As the pair sat around their campfire at dusk on the first evening, they heard the sound of tribal drums in the distance. The drums grew steadily louder. The guide took a deep breath and admitted: 'I don't like the sound of those drums.'

As darkness began to fall, the drums became louder still. The guide sighed: 'I really don't like the sound of those drums.'

As night fell, the drums were now so loud that they were obviously very near. The guide repeated ominously: 'I really do not like the sound of those drums.'

Just then the drums stopped and a voice from the darkness called out: 'Hey, man, he's not our regular drummer!'

What's the difference between a soprano and a terrorist?
– You can negotiate with a terrorist.

Stevie Wonder was playing his first-ever concert in Beijing and twenty minutes into the show, in a bid to strike up a rapport with his audience, he asked if anyone had any requests. At this, an old Chinese man in the front row shouted out: 'Play a jazz chord! Play a jazz chord!'

Stevie was impressed that the old man knew about the jazz influences in his career, and so he responded by playing an E minor scale before embarking on a complicated jazz melody that went on for over fifteen minutes.

When he finished, the rest of the audience applauded wildly, but the old man in the front row shouted out again: 'No, no, play a jazz chord! Play a jazz chord!'

Irritated that this one person was calling his jazz credentials into question, Stevie immediately launched into a brilliant jazz improvisation with his band around the B flat minor chord. Ten minutes later, he received a standing ovation – except from the old man in the front row who again shouted out: 'No, no. Play a jazz chord! Play a jazz chord!'

This was too much for Stevie to take. So he called out to the old man in the front row: 'Okay then, if you think you can do better, come up here and show everyone.'

The old man climbed slowly up on to the stage, tottered over to the microphone and started to sing: 'A jazz chord to say I love you . . .'

What's the difference between a violinist and a dog?
– A dog knows when to stop scratching.

A man was listening to a violin recital being given by his neighbour's son. At the end he said: 'Your son reminds me of Jamie Cullum.'

'I didn't know Jamie Cullum could play the violin,' said the neighbour.

'He can't,' said the man, 'and neither can your son!'

The Beach Boys walked into a bar.
    'Round?'
    'Round?'
    'Get a round.'
    'I get a round?'
    'Get a round . . .'

What is an accordion useful for?
– Learning how to fold a map.

Why are accordionists' fingers like lightning?
– They rarely strike the same spot twice.

How do you make a bandstand?
– Pull their chairs away.

What's the best way to tune a banjo?
– With wire cutters.

The world expert on wasps and the sounds they make was walking along the main street of a quiet country town when he stumbled upon an old record shop that sold vinyl classics. Flicking through the racks of LPs, his attention was caught by an album titled *Wasps of the World – and the Sounds They Make*.

Intrigued, he asked the young sales assistant if he could listen to the album.

'Certainly, sir,' said the assistant. 'Step into the booth, put on the headphones, and I'll put the LP on for you.'

So the world expert on wasps and the sounds they make stepped into the booth, put on the earphones and listened to the LP. Five minutes later, he came out of the booth and announced: 'I am the world expert on wasps and the sounds they make, but I didn't recognize any of those.'

'I'm very sorry, sir,' said the young assistant. 'If you'd like to step back into the booth, I'll play you another track.'

So the world expert on wasps and the sounds they make re-entered the booth and put the headphones back on. But five minutes later, he came out of the booth again, shaking his head. 'I don't understand it,' he said. 'I am the world expert on wasps and the sounds they make, and yet still I can't recognize any of those.'

'I really am sorry, sir,' said the young assistant. 'Perhaps if you would like to step back into the booth, I could play you another track.'

Eager to salvage his reputation, the world expert on wasps and the sounds they make went back into the booth, but emerged five minutes later in a state of considerable agitation. 'I am the world expert on wasps and the sounds they make, and yet I have recognized none of the wasps on this LP.'

'I really am terribly sorry,' said the young assistant, blushing. 'I've just realized I was playing you the bee side.'

Old People

An old man told the doctor: 'I don't know what's wrong with me. My right ear is always warmer than my left one.'

'I see the problem,' said the doctor. 'You need to adjust your toupee.'

An elderly couple died in a car crash. They had been in excellent health for years through taking regular exercise and also because the wife was obsessed with health foods, keeping a strict watch on both their diets.

So when St Peter welcomed them to Heaven,

they were keen to take advantage of the first-class relaxation facilities. The husband was particularly impressed by the eighteen-hole golf course and the Olympic-sized swimming pool.

'This really is an amazing place you've got,' he told St Peter.

'And there's more,' said St Peter. 'Let me show you the restaurant.'

As they observed the sumptuous buffet serving every food imaginable, the husband asked: 'Where's the low-fat table?'

'Oh, you don't have to worry about things like that anymore,' said St Peter. 'You can eat whatever you want here, no matter how fatty it is, and it's all free. That's the beauty of Heaven!'

With that, the husband threw his hat to the ground in a fit of temper.

'What's the problem?' asked St Peter.

Turning to his wife, the husband snapped: 'This is all your fault, Ethel. If it weren't for your goddam bran muffins, I could have been here ten years ago!'

A large, elderly woman was waiting at the side of the road. When a young man approached, she asked him: 'Can you see me across the road?'

He said: 'I can see you from half a mile away!'

An old lady phoned the police late one night and reported a sex maniac in her apartment.

'We'll be right over,' said the officer.

'Oh,' said the old lady, her voice tinged with disappointment. 'Can you wait until morning?'

A man went into a bank and withdrew five thousand dollars in cash. To keep the bills together, the bank teller bound them with a rubber band. Then the man stuffed the wad of money in his jacket pocket and exited the bank.

Five minutes later, he reached his car but found to his horror that the money was missing. He knew nobody had picked his pocket so he thought the bundle of bills must have somehow fallen from his pocket. He quickly retraced his steps to the bank where he collided with an elderly customer.

'Have you lost some money tied in a rubber band?' asked the old man.

'Yes, I have!'

'Well, I've found the rubber band.'

Two old men were talking about Viagra. One had never heard of it and asked the other what it was for.

'It's the greatest invention ever,' he said. 'It makes you feel like a man of thirty.'

'Can you get it over the counter?'

'Probably – if you took two.'

An elderly couple had been courting for over forty years and finally decided it was time they got married. But first they agreed they should work out the details of how their marriage was going to work in order to avoid any misunderstandings or disappointments.

So over dinner they had a long conversation about their future. They discussed finances, living arrangements, and all manner of things that affected them both. The old man took written notes of every point they covered. Finally he thought he should mention the physical side of their relationship.

'How do you feel about sex?' he asked tentatively, pencil in hand.

'Well,' replied the old lady, choosing her words carefully, 'I'd have to say . . . I would like it infrequently.'

The old man enquired: 'Is that one word or two?'

Two old men were sitting down to breakfast. One said to the other: 'Do you know you've got a suppository in your left ear?'

'Really?' said his friend, removing the suppository. 'I'm so glad you told me. Now I think I remember where I put my hearing aid.'

Two old men were sitting in the garden of their nursing home when a seagull flying overhead pooped on the bald head of one of the men.

The nurse who was in attendance said urgently: 'Don't worry, I'll run and fetch some toilet paper.'

As she hurried off, one old man turned to the other and said: 'Is she crazy or what? By the time she gets back with the toilet paper, that bird will be miles away!'

An elderly couple who had been courting for years finally decided to get married. While out making their plans, they stopped off at a drugstore.

The old man asked the sales assistant: 'Do you sell

pills for arthritis?'

'Yes, we do,' replied the assistant.

'What about heart medication?'

'Yes, we stock that, too.'

'Got anything for constipation?'

'Naturally, sir.'

'How about Viagra?'

'Yes, we sell Viagra.'

'Sleeping pills?'

'Yes, we stock a large selection of sleeping tablets.'

'Do you sell denture cleaner?'

'Of course we do, sir.'

'That's great!' exclaimed the old man, nodding to his bride-to-be. 'We'd like to register here for our wedding gifts.'

On a visit to see his grandma, a teenage boy listened to her complaining about the high cost of living.

'When I was a girl,' she said, 'you could go out with twenty cents and come back home with a dozen eggs, two pints of milk, a pound of bacon, half a pound of tea and a fresh chicken.'

'That's inflation for you,' he said.

'It's nothing to do with inflation,' she snapped. 'It's all the damn security cameras that shops have nowadays!'

A priest called on an elderly spinster at her home as part of his regular visits to his church members. While she went into the kitchen to make tea, he glanced around the lounge and began admiring a beautiful oak pump organ with a cut glass bowl sitting on top of it. The bowl was half filled with water and a condom was floating on the surface.

Stunned by the discovery, he was initially too embarrassed to mention it to the old lady but eventually his curiosity got the better of him and he felt compelled to ask her what it was doing there.

'Well,' she explained, 'when I was in town six months ago, I found a little foil package on the ground and brought it home. The directions on the back read, "Keep wet and put on your organ to prevent disease". And you know, I think it works! I haven't had a cold all winter!'

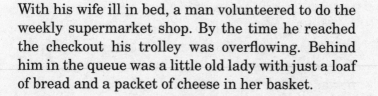

With his wife ill in bed, a man volunteered to do the weekly supermarket shop. By the time he reached the checkout his trolley was overflowing. Behind him in the queue was a little old lady with just a loaf of bread and a packet of cheese in her basket.

He turned to her and said: 'Is that all you've got, love?'

Her face lit up. 'Yes, dear,' she said.

'Well,' he said, 'if I were you, I'd have a sit-down, because I'm going to be ages here.'

Politicians

Arriving at church one morning, a preacher discovered a dead donkey in the church grounds. He called the police, but since there was no sign of foul play, the police referred him to the public health department. They said that as there was no obvious health threat, he should call the sanitation department. The manager there said he could not collect the dead donkey without authorization from the mayor. The preacher was reluctant to call the mayor, who was notoriously bad-tempered, but he realized that he had little choice.

The mayor was every bit as grumpy as the preacher had feared. 'What are you ringing me for?'

he bellowed. 'I've got better things to do with my time than worry about blasted donkeys. Anyway I thought it was your job to bury the dead.'

Unable to resist the temptation to retaliate, the preacher replied calmly: 'Yes, mayor, it is indeed my job to bury the dead, but first I always like to notify the next of kin!'

A council debate degenerated into a slanging match between the two rival parties. As matters became heated, one councillor sneered at an opponent: 'Have you actually heard of William Davies?'

'No,' admitted the other.

'Well,' said the first triumphantly, 'if you had taken the time to attend a few more council meetings, you would know that he is the man who is planning to open a new lap dancing club in the town.'

Stung into retaliation, the opponent responded: 'Have you ever heard of Kenneth Morris?'

'No,' said the first councillor. 'Who is he?'

'Well,' said the second, 'if you had attended fewer council meetings, you would know that he is the man who has been sleeping with your wife!'

A man was driving home from work when he found himself in a traffic jam, all the cars ahead having come to a halt. Just then he noticed a police officer approaching on foot.

'Do you know what the problem is, officer?' he asked.

The officer said: 'The city mayor is sitting in the middle of the road in a state of extreme agitation. He says he is deep in debt and is threatening to douse his body in gasoline and set fire to himself.'

'So what are you doing?'

'I'm going from car to car asking for donations,' replied the officer.

'How much have you collected so far?'

'Well,' said the officer, 'it's early days but already I've got seventeen gallons and many drivers are siphoning as we speak!'

Genuine Letters Sent To Council Offices

I wish to complain that my father hurt his ankle very badly when he put his foot in the hole in his back passage.

I am writing on behalf of my sink, which is running away from the wall.

Please send someone to mend our broken path. Yesterday my wife tripped and fell over and she is now pregnant.

Our lavatory seat is broken in half and is now in three pieces.

When the workmen were here they put their tools in my wife's new drawers and made a mess. Please send men with clean tools to finish the job and keep my wife happy.

I want some repairs doing to my cooker, as it has backfired and burnt my knob off.

When I applied for a rebate, you said that you would have to take something off. Now that you have taken it off, I have been told that you should have put some on. So will you please take off what you took off and put on what you should have put on when you took it off?

Could you please send a man to repair my spout? I am an old age pensioner and need it straight away.

I want to complain about the farmer across the road. Every morning at 5.30, his cock wakes me up, and it is getting too much.

The toilet is blocked and we cannot bath the children until it is cleared.

The person next door has a large erection in his back garden, which is unsightly and dangerous.

Please send a man to look at my water as it is a funny colour and is not fit to drink.

Our kitchen floor is very damp, we have two children and would like a third, so will you send someone to do something about it?

This is to let you know there is a smell coming from the man next door.

Sarah Palin was walking through the park one day when she saw a small boy carrying a box with air holes in the sides.

'What's in the box?' she asked.

'Kittens,' replied the boy. 'Brand new kittens. Only born yesterday.'

'And what type of kittens are they?' asked Palin.

'They're Republican kittens,' said the boy.

'That's lovely,' smiled Palin, and the boy ran off.

A few days later, Palin was out campaigning with

a party colleague when she spotted the same boy carrying his box of kittens. She went over to the boy, looked in the box and said: 'Aren't they cute? Tell my colleague here what type of kittens they are.'

'They're Democrat kittens,' replied the boy.

Palin was horrified. 'The last time I saw you, you told me they were Republican kittens! What's changed?'

The boy said: 'Their eyes are open now.'

Why don't politicians like golf?
– Because it's too much like their work: trapped in one bad lie after another.

The US government once owned a large scrapyard in the middle of the desert.

Congress said: 'Someone might steal from it at night.' So they created a nightwatchman position and hired a person for the job.

Then Congress said: 'How does the watchman carry out his job without instruction?' So they created a planning department and hired two people – one to write the instructions, and one to carry out time studies.

Then Congress said: 'How will we know if the night-watchman is doing his job properly?' So they created a quality control department and hired two people – one to do the studies and the other to write the reports.

Then Congress said: 'How are these people going to get paid?' So they created positions for a timekeeper and a payroll officer, then hired two people.

Then Congress said: 'Who will be accountable for all these people?' So they created an administrative section and hired three people – an administrative officer, an assistant administrative officer, and a legal secretary.

Then Congress said: 'We have had this command in operation for one year and we are twenty thousand dollars over budget. We must cut back on the overall cost.' So they laid off the nightwatchman.

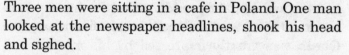

Three men were sitting in a cafe in Poland. One man looked at the newspaper headlines, shook his head and sighed.

Then the second man looked at his newspaper, shook his head and sighed.

The third man reached for his hat and said: 'If you two are going to discuss politics, I'm off.'

Psychiatrists

The Queen was paying an official visit to a psychiatric hospital. She talked to a male patient who was tending the hospital flowerbeds and asked him why he was there. In a calm and orderly manner, he told her his sad life story, adding that he had been in the institution for more than twenty-five years. The Queen was greatly impressed by his manner and hinted that she might be able to secure his release as he seemed completely cured and ready to resume his place in society. The man was extremely grateful and returned to his gardening duties as the Queen departed.

Her Majesty was just about to leave the hospital

grounds when a flying brick hit her on the back of the head. With blood oozing from the wound, she turned groggily to see the man standing there.

He said: 'You won't forget, will you?'

A man walked into a psychiatrist's office with a pancake on his head, a burger on each shoulder, a strip of bacon over each ear and a strand of spaghetti up his nose.

'How can I help you?' asked the psychiatrist.

The man said: 'I'm worried about my brother.'

A man told a psychiatrist: 'I think I'm a schizophrenic with multiple-personality disorder. Some days I believe I'm a temptress in a Bizet opera, other days I'm convinced that I am the head of the German Luftwaffe in the Second World War.'

The psychiatrist listened patiently before concluding: 'Well, it seems to me that you don't know if you're Carmen or Goering.'

Two psychiatrists passed in the corridor. The first said: 'Hello.'

The second thought: 'I wonder what he meant by that . . .'

A man told a psychiatrist: 'I have this recurring dream in which half a dozen beautiful women run into my bedroom and start tearing off my clothes.'

'What do you do?' asked the psychiatrist.

'I push them away.'

'I see. And how can I help you?'

'I want you to break my arms.'

A doctor was doing his rounds at a psychiatric hospital when he arrived at a room containing two patients. One patient was sawing an imaginary plank of wood while the other was hanging from the ceiling.

'What's he doing up there?' asked the doctor.

'He thinks he's a light bulb,' replied the patient who was doing the sawing.

'Shouldn't you get him down?' said the doctor. 'He might hurt himself.'

'What? And work in the dark?'

Did you hear about the man who suffered from paranoia and low self-esteem?
– He thought no one important was out to get him.

A man went to see a psychiatrist and said: 'I just can't seem to make friends. Can you help me, you fat slob?'

As part of her eventual rehabilitation, a patient at a mental hospital was told by the hospital psychiatrist to go out into the world and discover a new fact. After four hours, she returned to the hospital to tell the psychiatrist what she had learned.

First she put a large spider on his desk and shouted: 'Boo!' The spider scurried under the desk.

Then she picked up the spider, pulled off all its legs and shouted: 'Boo!' The spider couldn't move.

The psychiatrist scratched his head and said: 'I don't quite understand. What is it that you have learned?'

The patient replied: 'When I pull the legs off a spider, it can't hear me!'

A man walked into a psychiatrist's office and said: 'My wife thinks I'm crazy because I like sausages.'

'That's nonsense,' said the psychiatrist. 'I like sausages, too.'

'Great,' said the man. 'You must come and see my collection – I've got hundreds of them.'

A psychiatrist congratulated his patient on making excellent progress.

'You call this progress?' snapped the patient. 'Six months ago, I was Napoleon. Now I'm nobody!'

A psychiatrist conducted a test to determine whether a patient who had spent twenty years in an asylum was ready to cope with the outside world. For the test, the patient was taken to a movie theatre where half the seats bore a sign saying 'Wet Paint'. The psychiatrist was disappointed to see the patient choose one of the 'Wet Paint' seats but derived some comfort from the fact that he had the presence of mind to put a sheet of newspaper on the seat before sitting down.

Afterwards the psychiatrist said: 'Can I ask you why you chose one of the seats marked "Wet Paint"? There were plenty of other seats you could have sat on.'

'I like paint,' replied the patient.

'So why did you put a sheet of newspaper on the seat before sitting down?'

The patient replied: 'I thought I'd have a better view if I was sitting higher up.'

A young woman walked into a psychiatrist's office. He looked at her and said: 'Take off your clothes please and get on the couch.'

She was puzzled by the request but did as he asked. He then took off his pants and had sex with her on the couch.

'Right,' he said, zipping up his pants when he had finished, 'that's my problem solved. Now, what's yours?'

Why do psychiatrists give their patients shock treatment?
– To prepare them for the bill.

A young man who was chronically shy went into a bar and saw a beautiful woman sitting there. After an hour of plucking up courage, he finally went over to her and asked tentatively: 'Would you mind if I chatted to you for a while?'

She responded by yelling at the top of her voice: 'No! I won't sleep with you tonight!'

Everyone in the bar heard, leaving the poor young man embarrassed and bewildered. He slunk quietly back to his table, ready to leave as soon as he had finished his drink. But a few minutes later, the woman walked over to him and apologized.

'I'm really sorry if I embarrassed you,' she said. 'You see, I'm a graduate student in psychology, and I'm studying how people respond to embarrassing situations.'

To which the young man replied at the top of his voice: 'What do you mean, you charge two hundred dollars?!'

A man had become convinced that he was a dog, so he went to see a psychiatrist.

'It's terrible,' said the man, 'I walk around on all

fours, I keep barking in the middle of the night and I can't walk past a lamp post any more.'

'Very well,' said the psychiatrist. 'Get on the couch.'

The man said: 'I'm not allowed on the couch!'

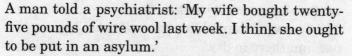

A man told a psychiatrist: 'My wife bought twenty-five pounds of wire wool last week. I think she ought to be put in an asylum.'

'Well,' said the psychiatrist, 'it's certainly an abnormally large amount to buy but it doesn't necessarily mean she's crazy.'

'Maybe not,' said the man. 'But then she started knitting a gas cooker.'

Melvin and Maureen were long-term patients in a psychiatric hospital. One day they were walking past the hospital swimming pool when, without warning, Melvin jumped into the deep end. Realizing he couldn't swim, Maureen dived in and dragged him to safety.

When the head psychiatrist heard about Maureen's heroism, he decided that she should be discharged from the hospital immediately as he considered her to be mentally sound. He went to inform her in person. 'Maureen,' he said, 'I have good and bad news. The good news is that I'm going to discharge you because you were able to jump into the pool and save the life of a fellow patient. On that basis, I believe you have finally regained your senses. The bad news is that Melvin, the patient you saved, subsequently hanged himself in the bathroom with the belt of his robe. I'm sorry to have to tell you he's dead.'

'Oh, no, he didn't hang himself,' said Maureen. 'I put him there to dry.'

A patient told his psychiatrist: 'I always have this weird dream at night. I am locked in a room, and there is this door with a sign on it. I try to push the door with all my strength, but no matter how hard I try it simply won't budge.'

'Interesting,' mused the psychiatrist. 'Tell me, what does the sign on the door say?'

The patient replied: 'It says "Pull".'

A woman walked into a psychiatrist's office and said: 'I need help. I think I could be a nymphomaniac.'

'Well, I might be able to help you,' said the

psychiatrist, 'but I must warn you that I charge one hundred dollars an hour.'

'That's fair,' said the woman. 'And how much do you charge for the night?'

A man phoned the psychiatrist at the local mental hospital and asked: 'Who's in Room Eighteen?'

'Nobody,' said the psychiatrist.

'Good,' said the man. 'I must have escaped.'

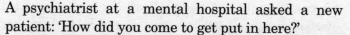

A psychiatrist at a mental hospital asked a new patient: 'How did you come to get put in here?'

'Well,' explained the patient, 'it all started when I got married. I married a widow with a grown-up daughter who therefore became my stepdaughter. Then one day my father came to visit, fell in love with my beautiful stepdaughter and married her. And so my stepdaughter was now my stepmother. Soon my wife had a son who was, of course, my father's brother-in-law since he was the half-brother of my stepdaughter who was my father's wife. Since my new son was brother to my stepmother, he also became my uncle. As you probably realize by now, my wife is also my step-grandmother because she is my stepmother's mother. Since I am married to my step-grandmother, I am not only my wife's grandson and husband, I am also my own grandfather! Now can you understand how I got put in this place . . . ?'

A married woman went to see a psychiatrist because she has having problems with her sex life. The psychiatrist asked her a series of questions but was no nearer finding a solution. Eventually he asked her: 'Do you ever watch your husband's face while you're having sex?'

'As a matter of fact,' she answered. 'I did once.'

'And how did he look?'

'Very, very angry.'

'I see,' said the psychiatrist, delighted that he finally appeared to be making progress. 'Well, that's extremely interesting. We must look into this further. Now tell me, you say you have only seen your husband's face once during sex. That is rather unusual. How did you come to see his face on that particular occasion?'

The wife replied: 'He was looking through the window at us.'

Peter and George were in a mental institution where the psychiatrist conducted an annual experiment to ascertain which patients were ready for release. He asked each patient two questions, and if they answered them correctly they were free to leave.

Peter was first to take the test. The psychiatrist asked him: 'What would happen if I poked out one of your eyes?'

'I'd be half blind,' said Peter.

'That's correct,' said the psychiatrist. 'What if I poked out both of your eyes?'

'I'd be completely blind.'

'Well done,' said the psychiatrist, and he shook Peter by the hand and told him he was free to go.

On his way out, Peter told George about the test and gave him the answers. Then George was called in to the psychiatrist's office.

'So,' began the psychiatrist, 'what would happen if I cut off your right ear?'

Remembering the answers Peter had fed him, George replied: 'I'd be half blind.'

The psychiatrist was puzzled but went on: 'And what would happen if I cut off your left ear?'

'I'd be completely blind,' said George.

'Why do you say you'd be blind if I cut off your ears?'

'Because', said George, 'my hat would fall over my eyes!'

What happens when a psychiatrist and a hooker spend the night together?

– In the morning each of them says: 'That's one hundred and fifty dollars please.'

A new receptionist started work in a psychiatrist's office. At the end of her first day, she asked the psychiatrist: 'How did I do?'

'Not too bad,' he said. 'But I would prefer it if in future you just said to callers, "We're really busy" rather than "It's a madhouse here".'

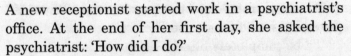

Two doctors – one a psychiatrist, the other a proctologist – opened an office in a small town and put up a sign reading: 'Dr Smith and Dr Jones: Hysterias and Posteriors'.

However the town council was not happy with the sign so the doctors changed it to 'Schizoids and Haemorrhoids'.

This was not acceptable either, so in an effort to appease the council they changed the sign to 'Catatonics and High Colonics'. Still it was rejected.

So they tried 'Manic Depressives and Anal Retentives'. Rejected. Their next idea, 'Minds and Behinds', was also turned down, as was 'Lost Souls and Butt Holes'.

So they tried 'Analysts and Anal Cysts', but that, too, fell foul of the council. 'Nuts and Butts', 'Freaks and Cheeks' and 'Loons and Moons' all met a similar fate.

Finally at their wits' end, the doctors came up with: 'Dr Smith and Dr Jones: Odds and Ends'. Everyone was happy.

Why is psychoanalysis a lot quicker for a man than for a woman?
– Because when it's time to go back to childhood, a man is already there.

A psychiatrist was just driving away from the asylum when he noticed he had a flat tyre. He removed the wheel but accidentally tipped over the hubcap containing the bolts, spilling them all down a sewer drain.

A patient, looking through the fence, suggested that the psychiatrist take one bolt from the remaining three wheels to hold the fourth wheel in place until he could get to a garage.

'That's an excellent idea,' said the psychiatrist. 'I don't know why you're in that place.'

The patient replied: 'I'm here for being crazy, not for being stupid.'

A woman went to see a male psychiatrist about her low self-esteem. She was alarmingly pale and obese. After she had tearfully explained her problems, the psychiatrist said: 'Right. Could you please lie on the floor under the window?'

The woman did as he asked.

'Now over by the door.'

She lay down near the door, as asked.

'And finally under the bookshelves. Thank you.'

As she lay on the floor beneath the bookshelves, he started making notes.

'You can get up now,' he said eventually.

'So can you help me?' she asked.

'Not really,' he said. 'Just get some pills from your doctor.'

'So what was all that stuff you had me doing, lying on the floor?'

'Oh, I'm having a new white sofa delivered next week and I was wondering where to put it.'

Rednecks

Having moved from Alabama, Billy-Bob was in his first day of grade three at his new school in Massachusetts. The teacher asked the class to count to fifty, which is about the standard for grade three. Most were able to count up to twenty, a few managed thirty, but Billy-Bob counted all the way up to a hundred with only one or two mistakes. After school, he ran home to tell his dad how well he had done. His dad said: 'That's because you come from Alabama, son.'

The next day, the teacher asked the class to recite the alphabet. Most got halfway, but Billy-Bob did it all with hardly any mistakes. After school, he ran home to tell his dad how well he had done. His dad said: 'That's because you come from Alabama, son.'

The next day after PE, the boys were taking

showers. Billy-Bob couldn't help noticing he was much better endowed than all the other boys in his grade. After school, he ran home to tell his dad.

'Is that because I'm from Alabama, Dad?'

'No, son, it's because you're eighteen.'

Billy-Bob and Bubba found three hand grenades and decided to take them to the nearest police station.

'What if one of them explodes before we get there?' asked Billy-Bob.

'Don't worry about it,' said Bubba. 'We'll just lie and tell them we only found two.'

What's a redneck's favourite pick-up line?
– 'Hey, nice tooth.'

A woman from Arkansas was in the welfare office filling out forms. The welfare officer asked her how many children she had.

'Nine boys,' she said.

'And what are their names?'

'Jed, Jed, Jed, Jed, Jed, Jed, Jed, Jed and Jed.'

'They're all named Jed? Why would you want to give all your kids the same name?'

'That way, when I wants them all to come in from the yard or for dinner, I just yells "Jed" and they all come.'

'But what if you want only one of them to do something.'

'Easy,' she said. 'I just calls him by his last name.'

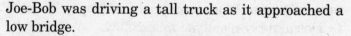

Joe-Bob was driving a tall truck as it approached a low bridge.

'Oh, no,' he said. 'The height of the bridge is nine foot and our truck is at least ten foot!'

'It's okay,' said Billy-Joe in the passenger seat. 'There's no cops around.'

Bubba was at the police station explaining to an officer why his cousin had shot him.

'We were having a real good time drinking,' said Bubba, 'when my cousin Billy-Bob picked up his rifle and asked if I wanted to go hunting.'

'Okay,' said the officer. 'Then what happened?'

Bubba replied: 'That's when I stood up and said, "Sure, I'm game."'

How many rednecks does it take to eat a possum?
– Two. One to eat the possum and the other to watch for traffic.

A stranger walked into a bar in Arkansas and ordered a gin and tonic. The bar fell silent. The bartender eyed him suspiciously and said: 'You ain't from round here, are you mister?'

'No,' said the stranger. 'I'm from Seattle.'

'Oh, yeah?' said the bartender. 'What d'you do up in Seattle?'

'I'm a taxidermist,' replied the stranger.

'A taxidermist, huh?' said the bartender. 'What's one of those?'

'I mount dead animals,' explained the stranger.

At this, the bartender called to the other drinkers: 'It's okay, boys. He's one of us.'

What do you call an Arkansas farmer with a sheep under each arm?
– A pimp.

You Know You're a Redneck When . . .

The value of your truck depends on how much gas there is in it.

You have five cars that are immobile and a house that isn't.

Your dad walks you to school because you're both in the same grade.

You mow your lawn and find a car.

Your wife's best shoes have steel toecaps.

Your gene pool doesn't have a deep end.

You've ever used lard in bed.

Your family tree doesn't fork.

Your Christmas stocking is full of ammo.

Wildlife is attracted to your beard.

Your mum's lost at least one tooth opening a beer bottle.

There's a gun rack on your bicycle.

You had to remove a toothpick for wedding pictures.

Your front porch collapses, and more than six dogs are killed.

Your wife weighs more than your fridge.

Your penknife has ever been referred to as 'Exhibit A'.

A tornado hits your neighbourhood and does half a million dollars of improvements.

Your dog passes gas and you claim it.

There's a wasps' nest in your living room.

The UFO hotline limits you to one call a day.

You own all the component parts of soap on a rope except the soap.

You own a special baseball cap for formal occasions.

You've ever been involved in a custody battle over a hunting dog.

A redneck patient was told by his doctor: 'Until the penicillin cleans out your infection, you ain't to have no relations whatsoever. Understand?'

'Yeah,' said the redneck, 'but what about friends and neighbours?'

Two Alabama State Troopers were chasing a suspect car towards Georgia. When the suspect crossed the Georgia line, the trooper who was driving pulled over to the side of the road.

'Why did you stop?' asked his colleague.

'Well, he's in Georgia now. They're an hour ahead of us, so we'll never catch him.'

Bubba was killed in a fire and suffered such severe burns that he was barely recognizable. So the undertaker called in Bubba's friends Jim-Bob and Joe-Bob so that the body could be formally identified.

Jim-Bob looked at the body and said: 'He sure is burnt to a crisp. Roll him over.'

The undertaker rolled the body over but Jim-Bob

said: 'That ain't Bubba.'

'Are you sure?' asked the undertaker.

'Yep,' said Jim-Bob. 'Call in Joe-Bob if you don't believe me.'

So Joe-Bob was brought in to identify the body. 'He sure is burnt,' said Joe-Bob, looking at the corpse's face. 'Roll him over.'

The undertaker rolled the body over again but Joe-Bob said: 'That ain't Bubba.'

The undertaker was mystified. 'How can you tell by rolling him over?'

'Because', they said, 'Bubba had two assholes.'

'What?!' exclaimed the undertaker.

'Yep, everyone round here knew. Every time the three of us went into town, people would say: "Here comes Bubba with them two assholes."'

A redneck boy ran into his house and announced excitedly: 'I've found the girl I'm gonna marry! And she's a virgin!'

His father thumped his fist on the table angrily. 'There's no way you're marrying that girl,' he yelled. 'If she ain't good enough for her own family, she sure ain't good enough for ours!'

What do a tornado and a redneck divorce have in common?
– Someone's gonna lose a trailer.

An Alabama state trooper pulled over a pickup truck on the highway.

He said to the driver: 'Got any ID?'

The driver replied: ''Bout what?'

How do you know you're at a redneck wedding?
– Everyone sits on the same side of the church.

How can you tell which is the groom at a redneck wedding?
– He's the one in the clean bowling shirt.

For the third time in two weeks, Joe-Bob was arrested for punching his wife. The judge asked: 'Why do you keep beating her?'

Joe-Bob said: 'I think it's my weight advantage, longer reach and superior footwork.'

Religion

Two nuns went on a shopping trip to France to load up with duty-free. On the way back they were just about to drive through 'Nothing to declare' when a customs officer waved them to the side.

The first nun said to the Mother Superior, who was driving: 'Don't worry. Just show him your cross.'

So the Mother Superior wound down the window, leaned out and shouted: 'Get lost, you bastard!'

Two Catholics were digging up the road opposite a brothel. One morning, they noticed a rabbi slip into the brothel. 'What is the world coming to,' they said, 'when a religious man enters a house of ill-repute?'

Twenty minutes later, they saw a Protestant minister sneak into the brothel. 'Dear oh dear!' they said. 'No wonder the world is in such a mess with this sort of thing going on.'

Twenty minutes later, they saw a priest creep into the brothel. 'Oh,' they said, 'one of the poor lasses must be ill.'

A teenage boy began dating a pretty Christian Fundamentalist and was keen to find out more about her religion. So he went to see the church elder. 'Tell me,' said the boy, 'does your religion permit the drinking of coffee?'

'No,' replied the elder. 'Coffee beans are specially treated to enhance their flavour, so we do not consider coffee to be wholly natural. We will not permit anything that is not natural.'

'What is the view on dancing?' asked the boy.

'We do not permit dancing', replied the elder, 'because it is unnatural.'

'What about sex?'

'Yes, sex is permissible provided it is between two people who are married.'

'What about kinky sex?'

'It depends what you mean by kinky sex.'

'Well,' said the boy, 'I was thinking about different positions, like standing up.'

'No,' said the elder gravely. 'It could lead to dancing.'

Patrick went into confessional and told the priest: 'Bless me, Father, for I have sinned. I have been with a loose woman.'

'Oh dear,' said the priest. 'Was it Siobhan Kelly?'

'No, Father,' said Patrick.

'Was it Mary O'Reilly?'

'No, Father.'

'Was it Bernadette Murphy?'

'No, Father.'

'Was it Angela Lynch?'

'No, Father.'

'Was it Niamh O'Hara?'

'No, Father.'

'Then was it Josephine Burke?'

'No, Father.'

A few minutes later, Patrick emerged from the confessional box and met his friend Mick.

'What did you get?' asked Mick.

Patrick said: 'Four Our Fathers, five Hail Marys, and six good leads.'

A priest offered a nun a ride home in his car. She climbed into the passenger seat and crossed her legs, offering the priest a revealing glimpse of flesh beneath her gown.

The priest was immediately overcome with lust and slyly slid his hand up her lower leg.

'Father!' said the nun. 'Remember Psalm 129.'

The priest removed his hand but when he next changed gear, he seized the opportunity to slide his hand up her lower leg again.

'Father!' repeated the nun. 'Remember Psalm 129.'

The priest apologized. 'I'm truly sorry, sister, but the temptation was too much. I am only human after all.'

Arriving at the convent, the nun sighed heavily and went on her way. When he reached his church, the priest rushed to look up Psalm 129. It said: 'Go forth and seek, further up, you will find glory.'

A highly agitated man ran through a crowded train calling out: 'Is there a Catholic priest on board?'

Receiving no reply, he ran through the train again, shouting: 'Is there an Anglican vicar on board?'

When nobody came forward, he became increasingly desperate and ran along the train yelling: 'Is there a rabbi on board?'

Finally a man caught his attention and said: 'Can

I be of any assistance? I'm a Methodist minister.'

'No, you're no use,' said the man. 'I'm looking for a corkscrew!'

Leaving church one Sunday, a middle-aged woman said to her husband: 'Do you think that O'Shaughnessy girl is dying her hair?'

'I didn't even see her,' replied the husband.

'And that skirt Mrs Kilkenny was wearing,' continued the wife. 'Don't tell me you thought that was appropriate attire for a thirty-seven-year-old mother of six?'

'I'm afraid I didn't notice that either,' said the husband.

'Huh!' scoffed the wife. 'A lot of good it does you going to church!'

A priest had his bicycle stolen and thought a member of his congregation was to blame. Seeking advice, he consulted his bishop who suggested: 'Why don't you give a sermon on the Ten Commandments? When you reach "Thou shalt not steal", look around and see who has a guilty expression. Then you'll know who the thief is.'

Two weeks later, the bishop met the priest and asked him whether the scheme had worked. 'Yes, it did,' said the priest, 'but not quite in the way you envisaged. You see, I was going through the Ten Commandments, one by one, and when I reached "Thou shalt not commit adultery", I remembered where I had left my bike!'

What do you call a nun with a washing machine on her head?
– Sistermatic.

Wanting to raise money for his church, a preacher decided to buy a racehorse. However at the auction the price was too high, so he had to settle for a donkey instead. The preacher figured that since he had bought the animal, he might as well race it, and to his delight the donkey finished third in its first race.

The next day's newspaper carried the headline: PREACHER SHOWS ASS.

The preacher was so pleased with the donkey that he decided to enter it in another race – this time at a big meeting – and it won.

The next day's newspaper read: HUNDREDS GATHER TO SEE PREACHER'S ASS.

However the bishop was so upset with these headlines that he ordered the preacher not to enter the donkey in any more races.

The following day, the newspaper ran the headline: BISHOP SCRATCHES PREACHER'S ASS.

This was too much for the bishop and he ordered the preacher to get rid of the donkey. The preacher decided to give the animal to a nun at a local convent.

The next day, the newspaper proclaimed: NUN HAS BEST ASS IN TOWN.

The bishop fainted.

When he came round, he informed the nun that she would have to dispose of the donkey. The nun eventually found a farmer who was willing to buy the animal for ten dollars.

The headline in the following day's newspaper read: NUN PEDDLES ASS FOR TEN BUCKS.

They buried the bishop the next day.

The Mother Superior called all the nuns together and announced: 'I must tell you all something. We have a case of gonorrhoea in the convent.'

'Thank heavens!' said an elderly nun at the back of the room. 'I'm so tired of Chardonnay.'

A young woman travelling home on a flight from England to the United States turned to the priest sitting next to her and said: 'Father, I wonder if I could ask you a favour?'

'Certainly, my dear,' he replied.

'When I was in London,' she said, 'I bought an expensive electronic hairdryer that is well over customs limits, and I'm worried they'll confiscate it. Would you mind carrying it through customs for me – under your robes perhaps?'

'I'd love to help you,' said the priest, 'and I will do what I can but I must warn you in advance: I will not lie for you.'

'Very well, Father. I understand. And thank you.'

When they arrived at Customs, she let the priest go through first. The customs official asked: 'Father, do you have anything to declare?'

The priest answered: 'From the top of my head down to my waist, I have nothing to declare.'

Puzzled by this response, the official asked: 'And what do you have to declare from your waist to the floor?'

The priest said: 'I have a marvellous little device designed to be used on a woman, but which is, to date, unused.'

The official smiled knowingly and said: 'Very good, Father. Go through. Next!'

You Know You're in a Bad Church When . . .

There's an ATM in the lobby.

The church bus has gun racks.

Communion is a two-drink minimum and there is a Happy Hour between six and seven every evening.

The choir is formed from the local chapter of Hell's Angels.

The church has a karaoke hymn machine.

Ushers ask, 'Smoking or non-smoking?'

The Bible they use is the Dr Seuss version.

The only song the organist knows is 'Livin' La Vida Loca'.

Many of the congregation are known to viewers of *America's Most Wanted*.

When the congregation are asked to stand, they automatically put their hands in the air.

Two nuns who worked in a hospital were out driving in the country when their car ran out of petrol. As they stood beside their car on the grass verge, a truck driver slowed down and asked if he could help. When the nuns explained that they had run out of petrol, he said he would gladly drain some from his tank but unfortunately he had neither a bucket nor a can.

So one of the nuns produced a clean bedpan from the trunk of their car and handed it to the trucker who proceeded to drain a couple of quarts of petrol into the pan. He then handed the bedpan to the sisters, climbed back into his truck and drove off.

While the nuns were carefully pouring the precious fuel into their petrol tank, a police officer happened to be passing by. Seeing them tipping in the contents of the bedpan, he smiled: 'I'm not sure that's going to work, sisters, but I admire your faith!'

A priest was walking through town when a woman wearing a short skirt approached him and said: 'Fancy a quickie for ten bucks?'

The priest replied: 'I don't know what you mean, my dear.' And he hurried on his way.

A little further down the street, he was accosted by another woman wearing heavy make-up. 'Fancy a quickie for ten bucks?' she asked.

'I have no idea what you're talking about,' said the priest. And he hurried on his way.

The incidents preyed on his mind, so he decided to drive out to the convent and call on the Mother Superior to discover whether she was familiar with the terminology.

The priest sat down with a nice cup of tea, and after exchanging the usual pleasantries he said to the Mother Superior: 'Tell me. What's a quickie?'

The Mother Superior answered: 'Ten bucks. The same as in town.'

What happened to the Pope when he went to Mount Olive?

– Popeye beat him up.

A bartender was busy behind the bar one lunchtime when two nuns walked in.

'Sisters,' he said, 'I'm surprised to see you here.'

'Why is that?' asked one of the nuns.

'Well, to be honest,' said the bartender, 'we don't get many nuns in here.'

The nun said: 'We minister to fallen souls, and thought that this would be a good place to find them.'

'Fair enough,' said the bartender, and he fetched them two iced waters.

Half an hour later, the bartender was going about his duties when two rabbis walked in. 'I'm really surprised to see you two here,' he said.

'Why is that?' asked one of the rabbis.

'Because, to tell the truth, we don't get a lot of rabbis in this bar.'

'The synagogue is closed for repairs,' explained the rabbi, 'and we needed somewhere quiet to debate rabbinical law.'

'Fair enough,' said the bartender, and he set them up with two orange juices.

Half an hour later, two Irish priests walked in. The bartender said: 'Fathers, I'm really surprised to see you two in here.'

One priest replied: 'Why is that, my son?'

The bartender said: 'Because you don't usually come in until the evening.'

An isolated monastery was inhabited by an order of monks who communicated with each other solely by chanting. Every morning, they would gather in the chapel and the abbot would chant: 'Good morning, assembled brethren.' And the monks would chant back: 'Good morning, Father Abbot.'

But one morning a maverick monk instead chanted: 'Good evening, Father Abbot.'

The abbot was not amused. Glaring at the monks, he declared: 'Someone chanted evening.'

A priest and a rabbi found themselves sharing a compartment on a train. Striking up a conversation, the priest said: 'I know that in your religion you're not supposed to eat pork. Have you actually ever tasted it?'

The rabbi replied: 'I must confess I have on the odd occasion.'

After a brief silence, the rabbi turned to the priest and said: 'I know that in your religion you're supposed to remain celibate. Have you ever had sex?'

The priest said: 'I must confess that I have succumbed once or twice.'

And the rabbi said: 'Better than pork, isn't it?'

In a bid to boost church attendance, a new Baptist minister began making personal calls to the homes of his parishioners. One man, who had not been to church for several months, was begged to join the congregation the following Sunday. He was a producer of fine peach brandy and, sensing an advertising opportunity, said that he would only attend church on condition that the pastor drank some of his brandy and, more importantly, admitted to doing so in front of his congregation. The pastor agreed and drank up.

That Sunday, as promised, the man attended the service and waited expectantly for the pastor to fulfil his part of the deal. After a few minutes, the pastor recognized him from the pulpit and declared with a smile: 'I note with pleasure that Mr Kennedy is here with us this morning. I want to thank him publicly for his hospitality this week and especially for the peaches he gave me and the spirit in which they were given.'

After his wife had given birth, the new church minister appealed to the congregation for a salary increase to cover the addition to his family. The congregation agreed that it was only fair, and approved it.

A year later, when his wife had another child, the minister again appealed to the congregation for a pay rise, and again they agreed to it.

Several years and five children later, the congregation had become a little concerned over the increased expenses. It turned into a showdown meeting with the minister at which tempers became frayed.

Eventually the minister stood up and shouted: 'Having children is an act of God!'

An elderly member of the congregation yelled back: 'So are rain and snow, but we wear rubbers for them!'

One morning, a crippled man hobbled into a Catholic church on crutches. He stopped in front of the holy water, rubbed some on both legs and threw away his crutches.

An altar boy witnessed the scene and ran into the rectory to tell the priest what he had just seen.

'Son, you've just witnessed a miracle!' said the priest. 'Tell me, where is this man now?'

'Flat on his backside over by the holy water,' said the boy.

What did the Virgin Mary say when she saw the three wise men?
– 'Huh, typical. You wait ages then three come at once.'

300

Twelve monks were about to be ordained. The final test meant that they had to line up naked while a nude model danced before them. Each monk had a small bell attached to his privates, and they were told that anyone whose bell rang would not be ordained because it meant he had not reached a state of spiritual purity.

The model danced before the first monk candidate but got no reaction. It was the same all the way down the line until she reached the final monk. As she danced provocatively in front of him, his bell rang with such force that it fell off and clattered to the ground. Embarrassed, he bent down to pick up the bell – and eleven other bells began to ring . . .

On a visit to a children's Sunday school, a new pastor observed proceedings and then asked the youngsters: 'Who tore down the walls of Jericho?'

'It wasn't me,' shouted young Timmy.

Unfazed by the comment, the pastor repeated: 'Come on now, who tore down the walls of Jericho?'

The teacher then took the pastor to one side. 'Look, Pastor, Timmy's basically a good boy. If he says he didn't do it, I believe him.'

The pastor couldn't believe what he was hearing and later that day relayed the story to the director of the Sunday school. The director frowned: 'I've heard Timmy can be a bit of a handful. I'll have a word with him.'

By now totally bemused, the pastor left and approached the deacon. Once again he told him the whole story, including the response of the teacher and the director.

The deacon listened patiently and smiled: 'Yes, Pastor, I can see your problem. But I suggest we take the money from the general fund to pay for the walls and leave it at that.'

Two nuns were ordered to paint a room in the convent but were under strict instructions from the Mother Superior that they were not to get as much as a speck of paint on their habits. So they decided to lock the door and paint the room in the nude.

They were halfway through painting the room when there was a knock on the door.

'Who is it?' called out one of the nuns.

'The blind man,' came the reply.

The two nuns looked at each other and, thinking that no harm could be done by letting a blind man enter the room, they opened the door.

'Right, sisters,' said the man. 'Where do you want these blinds?'

Bill was a regular visitor to his local racetrack, but he nearly always lost all his money. One day after failing to back a winner in the first three races, he noticed a priest step onto the track before the fourth race and bless the forehead of one of the horses at the starting stalls. Lo and behold, the horse, a rank outsider, went on to win the race.

So Bill was intrigued to see what the priest did before the start of the fifth race. Sure enough, the priest stepped out onto the track as the horses lined up and placed his blessing on the forehead of one of the horses. Convinced it was a good omen, Bill rushed to the window to put a small wager on the horse, and it duly romped home at a good price.

After collecting his winnings, Bill watched eagerly to see whether the priest would bless a horse before the sixth race. Right on cue, the priest stepped onto the track and blessed the forehead of one of the horses at the start. Bill quickly placed a larger bet and the horse – another long shot – raced to victory. Bill was elated that he had found the secret to success.

The same happened for the next three races, leaving Bill handsomely in profit. So before the last race of the day, he visited an ATM and withdrew his life savings. He then waited for the priest's blessing, which would tell him which horse to bet on. True to his pattern, the priest stepped onto the track and anointed the forehead, ears, eyes and hooves of one of the horses. Bill placed his bet – every cent he owned – then watched in despair as the horse trailed in last.

Dumbfounded, Bill sought out the priest. 'What happened, Father?' he demanded. 'All day you blessed horses and they won. The last race, you bless a horse and it loses. Now I've lost my life savings thanks to you!'

The priest nodded wisely and said: 'That's the trouble with you Protestants – you can't tell the difference between a simple blessing and the Last Rites.'

School

The schoolteacher asked Little Johnny if he knew his numbers.

'Yes,' he said. 'My dad taught me.'

'Good,' said the teacher. 'So what comes after eight?'

'Nine,' answered Johnny.

'And what comes after nine?'

'Ten.'

'And what comes after ten?'

'The jack.'

Little Johnny was late for school and said to the teacher: 'Sorry I'm late, miss, but I had to make my own breakfast this morning.'

'Very well, Johnny,' said the teacher, 'I'll accept your excuse but now that you're here, you can take part in our geography test. So, Johnny, do you know where the Scottish border is?'

'Yes, miss, in bed with my mum. That's why I had to make my own breakfast!'

Two female teachers accompanied a group of third, fourth and fifth graders on a field trip to the local racecourse to learn about thoroughbred racehorses. During the tour some of the children needed to go to the toilet, so it was decided that the girls would go with one teacher while the boys went with another.

As the teacher assigned to the boys waited outside the men's toilet, one of the boys came out and told her that he couldn't reach the urinal. Reluctantly the teacher went inside and began hoisting the little boys up by their armpits, one by one. As she lifted one up by the armpits, she couldn't help noticing that he was unusually well endowed for an elementary school child.

'I guess you must be in the fifth?' she said.

'No, ma'am,' he replied. 'I'm in the seventh, riding Linda's Legacy. Thanks for the lift anyway.'

Little Johnny's father said: 'Can I see your school report?'

'I haven't got it,' said Johnny.

'Why not?'

'My friend Kenny borrowed it. He wants to scare his parents.'

Arriving home from school, Little Johnny told his mother: 'My teacher thinks I'm going to be famous.'

'Really?' said his mother. 'Why? What did she say?'

'She said all I have to do is mess up one more time and I'm history!'

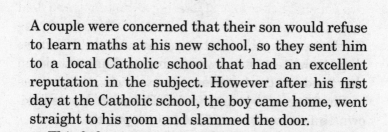

A couple were concerned that their son would refuse to learn maths at his new school, so they sent him to a local Catholic school that had an excellent reputation in the subject. However after his first day at the Catholic school, the boy came home, went straight to his room and slammed the door.

This behaviour continued every school night for the next six weeks, at the end of which his parents were invited along to meet the teachers. They feared the worst but instead their son's maths teacher revealed that the boy was top of the class.

On their way home, they asked their son: 'So what changed your mind about learning maths? You used to hate the subject.'

'Well,' said the boy, 'on the first day I walked into the classroom, I saw a guy nailed to a plus sign at the back of the room, so I knew straight away that they meant business!'

The teacher called Little Johnny to her desk. She told him: 'This essay you've written about your pet dog is word for word exactly the same essay as your brother has written.'

'Of course it is,' said Johnny. 'It's the same dog!'

For homework, the teacher asked each child in her class to write a story with a moral. The next day, they read out their stories.

First to go was young Rachel. She said: 'My daddy owns a farm and every Sunday we put the chicken eggs on the truck and drive to town to sell them at market. But one Sunday we hit a pothole in the road and all the eggs smashed. And the moral of the story is: don't put all your eggs in one basket.'

'That's very good, Rachel,' said the teacher. 'Now it's your turn, Alice.'

Alice read out her story. 'My daddy also owns a farm. Every weekend we take the chicken eggs and put them in an incubator. Last weekend, only six of the ten eggs hatched. And the moral of the story is: don't count your chickens until they're hatched.'

'Well done, Alice,' said the teacher. 'Now let's hear your story, Johnny.'

Little Johnny read out his story. 'My grandad fought in Vietnam, but one day his plane was shot down. He parachuted to safety before it crashed but he could only take with him a case of beer, a machine gun and a machete. He drank the case of beer on the way down and landed in the middle of thousands of enemy soldiers. He shot sixty-five Vietcong with the gun and when he ran out of bullets he killed another twenty with his machete and throttled twelve more with his bare hands.'

'That's a remarkable adventure,' said the teacher, 'but what is the moral of the story?'

Johnny said: 'Don't mess with my grandad when he's drunk.'

A young girl came home from school and said: 'Mummy, today in school I was punished for something I didn't do.'

'That's terrible,' said the mother. 'I'm going to speak to your teacher about it. Now what was it that you didn't do?'

The girl replied: 'My homework.'

On the first day of the new academic year, the school secretary was filling out forms relating to each student's personal details,

'What is your father's occupation?' she asked a new boy at school.

'He's a magician,' replied the boy.

'A magician! How interesting! What's his favourite trick?'

'He saws people in half.'

'Gosh! That's amazing! Now, next question. Any brothers or sisters?'

'Yes. One half-brother and two half-sisters.'

Little Johnny's mother was puzzled why he was home from school early.

'I was the only one who could answer a question,'

replied Johnny.

'Really?' said his mother. 'What was the question?'

'Who set Miss Hamilton's dress on fire?'

Genuine Student Bloopers

Nitrogen is not found in Ireland because it is not found in a free state.

The alimentary canal is located in the northern part of Indiana.

H_2O is hot water and CO_2 is cold water.

When you smell an odourless gas, it is probably carbon monoxide.

A kangaroo keeps its baby in the porch.

The Greeks invented three kinds of columns – Corinthian, Doric and Ironic.

Homer also wrote the 'Oddity', in which Penelope was the last hardship that Ulysses endured on his journey. Actually, Homer was not written by Homer but by another man of that name.

Marie Curie did her research at the Sore Buns Institute in France.

Television was invented by a Scotsman named John Yogi Bear.

Romeo and Juliet were star-crossed lovers, which means they were both cross-eyed.

William Shakespeare was born in the year 1564, on his birthday.

Abraham Lincoln's mother died in infancy, and he was born in a log cabin which he built with his own hands.

Johann Bach wrote a great many musical compositions and had a large number of children. In between he practised on an old spinster which he kept in his attic.

Henry VIII found walking difficult because he had an abbess on his knee.

Louis Pasteur discovered a cure for rabbis.

Benjamin Franklin died in 1790 and is still dead.

A boy was doing his geography homework one evening when he turned to his father and asked: 'Dad, where are the Andes?'

'Don't ask me,' said the father. 'Ask your mother. She puts everything away in this house.'

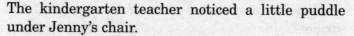

The kindergarten teacher noticed a little puddle under Jenny's chair.

'Oh, Jenny!' said the teacher. 'You should have put your hand up.'

'I did,' said Jenny, 'but it still trickled through my fingers.'

Little Johnny's father was disappointed that the boy scored such low marks in a school spelling test.

'Why did you get such a bad mark?' he asked.

'Absence,' said Little Johnny.

'What do you mean? Were you absent on the day of the test?'

'No,' said Little Johnny, 'but the boy who sits next to me was!'

One day at school, the teacher decided to play an animal game. She held up a picture of a giraffe and asked if any of the class knew what it was. 'See its long neck?' she said. 'What animal has a long neck?'

And Jenny answered: 'It's a giraffe.'

'Very good, Jenny,' said the teacher.

Then the teacher held up a picture of a zebra, and when no answers were forthcoming, she said: 'See the stripes on this animal? What animal has stripes?'

And Timmy answered: 'It's a zebra.'

'Well done, Timmy,' said the teacher.

Next the teacher held up a picture of a deer. None of the children recognized the animal, so the teacher said: 'See the big antlers on this animal? What animal has horns?'

Still nobody put up their hand, so the teacher offered a further clue: 'It's something your mother calls your father.'

Little Johnny immediately shouted out: 'I know what it is. It's a horny bastard.'

Sex

A woman was having an affair while her husband was out at work. One day she was in bed with her boyfriend when she heard her husband's car pull into the driveway.

'Quick!' she shouted to her boyfriend. 'Grab your clothes and jump out the window. My husband is home early!'

The boyfriend looked out the window and said: 'I can't jump! It's raining like crazy out there and I'm naked!'

'I don't care,' she insisted. 'If my husband catches us, he'll kill the pair of us.'

So the boyfriend grabbed his clothes and jumped from the bedroom window. When he landed, he found himself in the middle of a group of marathon runners. Hoping to blend in even though he was naked, he started running alongside them, carrying his clothes over his arm.

One of the runners asked: 'Do you always run in the nude?'

Thinking on his feet, the boyfriend replied breathlessly: 'Yes, always. It feels so free having the air blow over my skin while I'm running.'

'Do you always run carrying your clothes on your arm?' queried the athlete.

'Oh yes,' panted the boyfriend. 'That way I can get dressed at the end of the run, get in my car and just go straight home without a shower.'

'And', the athlete added, 'do you always wear a condom when you run?'

'Only if it's raining.'

A boy was brought up by very strict parents who never allowed him to meet girls. He was so naïve that when one day he saw a school friend kissing a girl, he went straight home to his mother and asked her what they were doing.

His mother told him: 'It's called kissing, and any boy that does that to a girl will be instantly turned to stone!'

On the boy's twenty-first birthday, he was introduced by a friend to a sweet girl who knew that he had never been kissed before. When she got him alone, she tried to kiss him, but he resisted.

'Why won't you let me kiss you?' she asked. 'There's nothing to be afraid of.'

'There is!' he said. 'My mother says that if I kiss a girl, I'll die that very minute!'

'That is nonsense,' said the girl, and she proceeded to plant a full kiss on his lips.

He instantly recoiled in horror. 'Oh no, I'm going to die!' he exclaimed.

'No you're not,' she said.

'I am,' he insisted. 'I've only just kissed you and already one part of me has started to get stiff!'

Two men were discussing their marriages. One said: 'I slept with my wife before we were married. Did you?'

'I don't know,' said the other. 'What was her maiden name?'

A wife was standing in the kitchen one morning, preparing soft-boiled eggs and toast for breakfast, and wearing only the T-shirt she had slept in. As her husband walked in, she turned to him and said: 'I need you to make love to me right now, here, across the kitchen table.'

Before she could change her mind, he had sex with her on the kitchen table.

Afterwards, she hurriedly thanked him and returned to the stove.

Happy but puzzled, he asked her: 'What was all that about?'

'Oh,' she said. 'The egg timer's broken.'

Sex Is Like . . .

Riding a bike – you have to keep pumping if you want to get anywhere.

Your salary – you don't disclose what you get but you always think others are getting more.

A pack of Pringles – once you pop, you just can't stop.

Air – it's no big deal unless you aren't getting any.

Golf – you can enjoy it without being any good at it.

Snow – you never know how many inches you're going to get or how long it's going to last.

Money – only too much is enough.

Pizza – when it's good, it's really good; when it's bad, it's still kinda good.

Art – most of it is pretty bad and the good stuff is out of your price range.

Playing bridge – if you don't have a good partner, you'd better have a good hand.

Fractions – it is improper when the larger one is on top.

Mathematics – add the bed, subtract the clothes, divide the legs and multiply.

Two guys were driving along when they saw a pair of dogs mating in a front garden. The driver remarked: 'That's great! My wife and I do that every night.'

The passenger said: 'My wife is more conservative – she likes the old-fashioned way. But if you tell me how you get your wife to do that, I'll give it a try.'

'It's easy,' said the driver. 'I just pour her a couple of martinis and she's game for anything.'

'Okay,' said the passenger. 'I'm going to try that tonight.'

When the two men met the following morning, the driver asked: 'So how did you get on last night?'

'It was amazing,' said the passenger, 'but it took my wife ten martinis.'

'Ten martinis?'

'Yeah, after two she was more than willing to make love that way, but it took eight more to get her out on the front lawn.'

Why don't women blink during foreplay?
– They don't have time.

A couple were desperate for sex but with a nine-year-old son around, they never had any time to themselves. So one day, they devised a plan where they sent him out onto the balcony of their high-rise apartment and asked him to report on everything that was going on in the neighbourhood while they enjoyed a quickie inside.

The boy stood on the balcony as instructed and

reported on everything that was happening. 'A police car has just called at the Browns' house, the Pearces have just had a new TV delivered, and the Kennedys are having sex.'

Hearing this, the boy's parents stopped in their tracks. 'How do you know the Kennedys are having sex?'

'Because their kid is standing on the balcony, too.'

Tom worked so hard that his only relaxation in life was going bowling two nights a week. His wife became so concerned about him overdoing it at the office that for his birthday she took him to a local strip club.

The club doorman greeted them. 'Hey, Tom, how are you doing?'

His wife was puzzled by this and asked Tom whether he had ever been to the club before.

'No,' said Tom. 'The guy's on my bowling team.'

When they sat down, a waitress asked Tom if he wanted his usual and brought over a Budweiser.

His wife grew increasingly uncomfortable. 'How did she know you drink Budweiser?' she asked.

'Oh,' said Tom, 'she's in the ladies' bowling league. We share lanes with them.'

A stripper then came over to their table, threw her arms around Tom, rubbed herself all over him and said: 'Hi, Tommy. Want your usual table dance, big boy?'

Tom's wife, now furious, grabbed her handbag and stormed out of the club. Tom followed, and spotted her getting into a cab. Before she could slam the door, he jumped in beside her and tried to explain how the stripper must have mistaken him for someone else. But his wife was having none of it. Instead she screamed at him at the top of her voice, calling him every insult in the book.

Hearing the row, the cab driver turned around and said: 'Gee, Tom, you picked up a real bitch this time!'

A cowboy walked into a barber's shop, sat in the chair and said: 'I'll have a shave and a shoe shine.'

While the barber began to lather the cowboy's face, a beautiful woman knelt down and started to shine his shoes. The cowboy was so impressed by her magnificent figure and long flowing hair that he said: 'Young lady, you and I should have wild sex in a hotel room tonight.'

'I'm married,' she answered, 'and I don't think my husband would approve.'

'Well,' said the cowboy, 'make up an excuse. Tell him you're working late.'

'You tell him,' she said. 'He's the one shaving you.'

A circus advertised for a new lion tamer. There were two applicants – a young man and a beautiful girl.

At the audition the circus owner warned them: 'This is one ferocious lion. He ate my last tamer and mauled the one before that, so you'd better be good. All the equipment you'll need is over there – a chair and a whip. So who wants to go first?'

The girl volunteered, completely ignored the whip and calmly stepped into the lion's cage where she sat down on the chair. As the lion bounded menacingly toward her, she threw open her coat to reveal that she was stark naked underneath. The lion immediately stopped in its tracks, rolled over on its back and began rubbing its head affectionately on her legs.

The circus owner was amazed. Turning to the young man, he said: 'Well, can you top that?'

'Sure I can,' said the young man, 'if you get that damn lion out of the way!'

With his wife eight months' pregnant, a man was becoming increasingly desperate for sex. One night as he gazed at her in frustration, she finally took pity on him, reached into a drawer and said: 'Here, take this fifty-dollar bill to the woman at number twenty-eight. She will let you sleep with her. But remember, this is a one-off. Don't even think about trying it again.'

'Thanks, honey,' he said, and rushed out of the door before she changed her mind.

A few minutes later, he returned, handed the bill back to his wife and said dejectedly: 'It's not enough. She says she wants sixty.'

'That bitch!' raged the wife. 'When she was pregnant and her husband came over here, I only charged him fifty!'

What happened when the chef got his hand caught in the dishwasher?
– They both got fired.

A sex therapist asked a man: 'Do you talk to your wife while you are having sex?'

He replied: 'Only if there's a phone handy.'

Things Not To Say During Sex

I hope you're as good-looking when I'm sober.

Have you got any penicillin?

Keep the noise down. Mother's a light sleeper.

But everybody looks funny naked!

Is that blood on the headboard?

It makes a change being with a woman I don't have to inflate.

You're almost as good as my ex.

Maybe we can try again later.

Did you ever see . . . ?

I thought you had the keys to the handcuffs!

Did you remember to lock the back door?

Did I tell you my Aunt Ethel died in this bed?

Is that it?

A man complained to his doctor that his sex life had become boring. So the doctor advised him to inject a little spontaneity into the relationship and take his wife by surprise with an unexpected demonstration of passion. The man thought it sounded a good idea.

A week later, he returned to the doctor and said: 'I did everything you suggested. I left work early without telling my wife, dashed into the house and found my wife in the living room. Without saying a word, I immediately stripped her naked and made wild, passionate love to her on the coffee table.'

'And was it good?' asked the doctor.

'It was fantastic,' said the man, 'although I'm not sure the Bible group were too impressed!'

A professor was invited to give a talk to a women's lunch group on sex. But because he was embarrassed about his wife knowing, he told her that the subject of his talk was horse riding.

A few days later, his wife ran into two members of the group at the supermarket. They complimented her on the speech her husband had made.

'Yes, I heard,' she said. 'But I was surprised about the subject matter because he's only tried it twice. The first time he got so sore he could hardly walk and the second time he fell off!'

Tarzan had been living alone in the jungle for over twenty years and during that time had been forced to use suitable shaped holes in trees for sex. Then one day, Jane showed up, just as Tarzan was thrusting himself into the hole of an oak tree.

'You can't carry on like that,' said Jane. 'Here, take me instead.'

As Jane reclined seductively on the grass, an already aroused Tarzan ran over to her and kicked her hard in the crotch.

'What did you do that for?' asked Jane.

Tarzan replied: 'Tarzan always check for squirrels first.'

A woman went into a bar in Texas and saw a cowboy with his feet propped up on a table. He had the biggest feet she had ever seen. She asked him if it's true what they say about men with big feet.

The cowboy grinned and said: 'Sure is, little lady. Why don't you come on out to the bunk house and let me prove it to you!'

The woman wanted to find out for herself, so she spent the night with him. The next morning she handed him a hundred-dollar bill.

Blushing, he said: 'Why thank you, ma'am. I'm flattered. Nobody's ever paid me for my services before.'

'Don't be flattered,' she said icily. 'Take the money and buy yourself some boots that fit!'

A little boy woke up three nights in a row when he heard a thumping sound coming from his parents' bedroom. Finally one morning he said to his mother: 'Mum, every night I hear you and Daddy making a noise and when I look in, you're bouncing up and down on him.'

'Oh,' said his mother, searching desperately for an explanation, 'I'm bouncing on his stomach because he's fat and that makes him thin again.'

'It won't work,' said the boy.

'Why not?'

'Because the lady next door comes by after you leave each day and blows him back up!'

George was walking along the street when he saw his friend Bill pull up in a Rolls-Royce. 'Hey, Bill,' he said. 'Where did you get a car like that?'

Bill said: 'You won't believe it when I tell you. I was

in town yesterday when a beautiful brunette pulled up in this car and offered me a lift. So naturally I accepted, and as soon as I got in she started kissing me. Then she drove to a quiet country lane, dragged me into the back seat, took off all her clothes except her black lacy knickers and purred: 'Take what you want.'

'What did you do?' asked George.

'Well,' said Bill, 'I could see her underwear wouldn't fit me, so I took the car.'

Pinocchio's girlfriend kept complaining: 'Every time we make love I get splinters.'

So Pinocchio sought the advice of his maker, Gepetto the carpenter. 'What you need, Pinocchio,' said Gepetto, 'is sandpaper. That will solve the problem.'

So Pinocchio bought some sheets of sandpaper. A few weeks later, Gepetto bumped into Pinocchio in the street. 'How are you getting on with the girls since you started using the sandpaper?' he asked.

Pinocchio said: 'Who needs girls?'

An insecure young man asked his girlfriend how she would describe him as a lover.

'Warm,' she replied. 'Yes, that's the word I'd use: warm.'

He was flattered until he went home and, out of interest, looked up the meaning of the word 'warm' in the dictionary.

His face fell as he read: 'Warm: not so hot.'

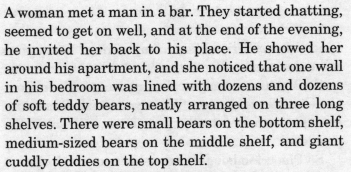

A woman met a man in a bar. They started chatting, seemed to get on well, and at the end of the evening, he invited her back to his place. He showed her around his apartment, and she noticed that one wall in his bedroom was lined with dozens and dozens of soft teddy bears, neatly arranged on three long shelves. There were small bears on the bottom shelf, medium-sized bears on the middle shelf, and giant cuddly teddies on the top shelf.

'What's with the teddies?' she asked.

'Oh, I used to work in a fairground,' he replied, 'and besides I think they're kinda cute.'

Impressed by having met such a sensitive man, she kissed him tenderly on the lips. He responded, and they fell into bed, where they proceeded to have sex.

Afterwards, she rolled over and, gently stroking

his chest, asked him: 'Well, how was it?'

Avoiding eye contact, he said brusquely: 'Help yourself to any prize from the bottom shelf.'

A couple had been married for twenty years, during which time the husband always insisted on turning off the light before making love. His wife eventually became so fed up with the routine that one night while they were in the middle of having sex, she suddenly turned the light back on. She looked down to see that he was holding a vibrator.

She exploded with rage. 'You've been cheating me all these years,' she screamed. 'You liar! You'd better explain yourself!'

'Okay,' he said calmly. 'I'll explain the sex toy. You explain our four kids!'

A man was desperate for sex but he only had seven dollars. He was thrown out of the first two whorehouses he went to, so he tried a third.

'I need sex,' he told the Madame. 'But I've only got seven dollars.'

'That's not much,' she said, 'but for seven dollars we can give you a penguin.'

'What's a penguin?' he asked.

'You'll see,' she said.

So he paid his seven dollars, went upstairs and waited for his penguin. A few minutes later a young woman came in and started giving him hand relief. But at the last moment, she suddenly stopped and walked away. Frustrated beyond belief, he waddled after her with his pants around his ankles, screaming: 'What's a penguin?'

She was only . . .

. . . a photographer's daughter, but she was really well developed.

. . . a road worker's daughter, but she knew how to get her asphalt.

. . . a barrister's daughter, but she kept a tight hold of her briefs.

. . . a draughtsman's daughter, but she knew where to draw the line.

. . . a constable's daughter, but she wouldn't let the Chief Inspector.

. . . a weatherman's daughter, but she had a warm front.

. . . a doctor's daughter, but she really knew how to operate.

. . . a jockey's daughter, but all the horse manure.

. . . an optician's daughter, but she was always making a spectacle of herself.

. . . a fisherman's daughter, but all the guys swallowed her lines.

. . . an electrician's daughter, but she was well connected.

. . . a bookbinder's daughter, but she knew her way between the sheets.

. . . a violinist's daughter, but when she took off her G-string all the boys fiddled.

. . . a minister's daughter, but I wouldn't put anything pastor.

. . . a whisky maker's daughter, but he loved her still.

. . . a florist's daughter, but she had the best tulips in town.

. . . a plumber's daughter, but she sure gave my heart a wrench.

. . . a cattleman's daughter, but she couldn't keep her calves together.

. . . a gravedigger's daughter, but anyone cadaver.

. . . a barman's daughter, but she knew how to pull without getting stout.

Shopping

A man went into a hardware store and asked for some nails.

'How long do you want them?' asked the assistant.

'Oh,' said the customer. 'I was rather hoping to keep them.'

On a trip to a shopping mall, a couple agreed to split up, visit their favourite shops and meet up again in an hour and a half. So while the husband visited the camera shop and the bike shop, his wife targeted the big clothes store. When he met up with her ninety minutes later as arranged outside the store, she was carrying a dozen bags filled with clothes.

'I don't believe it!' he exclaimed. 'Have you really bought all that?'

'Well, yes,' she replied. Then gesturing towards the interior of the shop, she added: 'But look at all the stuff I'm leaving behind.'

A man went to the perfume counter of a big department store and said he wanted a bottle of Chanel No. 5 gift-wrapped for his wife's birthday.

'A little surprise, is it?' asked the sales assistant.

'Yes,' said the man. 'She's expecting a new car!'

A woman was out Christmas shopping with her three young children. After hours of trailing around toyshops and hearing her kids asking for every item on the shelves, she was thoroughly fed up. Weighed down with bags, she squeezed herself and her kids into a crowded shopping mall elevator and sighed aloud, to nobody in particular: 'Whoever started this whole Christmas thing should be arrested and strung up!'

A voice from the back of the elevator replied quietly: 'Don't worry, ma'am, I believe they crucified him.'

A man bought a second-hand rug online but when it arrived he was horrified to see there was a large hole in the middle. He immediately contacted the seller to protest about the state of the rug.

The seller emailed him back: 'Well, I did say it was in mint condition.'

A man went into a discount store and asked the woman at the cash desk if everything in the store really was only one dollar.

'That's right,' she said. 'Every item in the store.'

So he gave her a dollar and asked for the cash register.

A store manager overheard a sales assistant saying to an elderly customer: 'No, madam, we haven't had any for some weeks now, and it doesn't look as if we'll be getting any soon.'

Alarmed by what he was hearing, the manager rushed over to the customer as she was exiting the store and said: 'I'm sorry, madam, you were given incorrect information. Of course we'll have some soon. In fact, we placed an order for it earlier this week.'

Then the manager pulled the sales assistant to one side and growled: 'Never, ever say we don't have something. If we haven't got it, say we ordered it and we're expecting it any day. Do you understand? Now what was it she wanted?'

The assistant said: 'Rain.'

A woman walked up to the cash desk in a clothes store carrying a pack of white sports socks. She said to the sales assistant: 'Would you mind opening the pack so that I can feel how soft the socks are?'

Reluctantly the assistant tore open the package, allowing the woman to examine the socks. Eventually she said, 'Yes, these are fine', and handed the pack back to the assistant.

But as the assistant started to ring up the sale on the cash register, the woman said: 'No, I don't want that pack! It's been opened.'

A man called in to a twenty-four-hour grocery store just as the owner was locking up.

'Hey,' said the man. 'Your sign says you're open twenty-four hours.'

'We are,' replied the owner, 'but not all at once.'

A man was browsing around a magic shop looking for a novelty gift when the shop owner went over to him and said: 'I've got just the thing for you, sir – magic glasses. They cost eight hundred dollars but they're worth it because when you wear them, you can see people naked. Here, try them on.'

So the man put on the magic glasses and, sure enough, the shop owner appeared naked. And when his pretty young assistant walked by, she was naked, too. When he removed the glasses, everybody was fully clothed.

'These are great,' said the man. 'I'll buy them.'

Wearing the glasses, he left the shop and headed back to his place of work. Everybody he passed in the street was naked – old men, young women and police officers alike – and he was so thrilled with his purchase that he decided to surprise his wife at home before returning to the office.

He was still wearing the glasses when he entered the living room where his wife and a male neighbour were sitting on the sofa completely naked. As they recoiled in horror at being discovered, the husband laughed: 'I can see you naked!' He then took off the glasses, but they were still naked.

'Well, I'll be damned!' he groaned. 'Eight hundred dollars for a pair of magic glasses – and after only half an hour they're broken!'

A man went to a store to buy a chimney. 'How much is this one?' he asked.

'Oh,' replied the sales assistant, 'it's on the house.'

Two lions were walking down the aisle of a supermarket. One turned to the other and said: 'Quiet in here today, isn't it?'

A rough woman took her four-year-old son shopping but when they arrived home, she was surprised to find a chocolate bar in his pocket.

'Where did you get this bar of chocolate?' she yelled. 'You didn't buy it and I didn't buy it! Have you been stealing?'

The boy hung his head in shame.

'Right,' she said, grabbing his coat, 'we're going straight back to the shopping mall . . . but this time we're calling in at the jewellers!'

A customer walked into a downtown hardware store and asked the manager: 'Do you have any brackets?'

'No, sorry.'

'Well, do you have any screwdrivers?'

'No, I'm afraid we're out of those, too.'

'What about hammers? Do you have any hammers?'

'Sorry, no.'

'Pliers?'

'No.'

'Spanners?'

'No.'

'Door handles?'

'No.'

'This is a total waste of time!' raged the customer. 'If you don't have anything in stock, you might as well lock up the damn shop!'

'I can't,' said the manager. 'I don't have a key.'

Sport

American Football

The coach of a college football team walked into the locker room before a game, turned to his star player and said: 'I'm not supposed to let you play since you failed maths, but we need you out there. So I'm gonna ask you a maths question, and if you get it right you can play.'

The player agreed, and the coach looked intently into his eyes and said: 'Okay, now concentrate. What is two plus two?'

The player thought for a moment and answered: 'Four.'

'Four!' the coach exclaimed, excited that he had got it right.

At that, all the other players on the team began yelling: 'Come on coach, give him another chance!'

A freshman built like a human colossus tried out for the college football team.

'Can you tackle?' asked the coach.

'Sure I can,' said the freshman, and he proceeded to run straight into a telephone pole, shattering it into splinters.

'Pretty impressive,' nodded the coach. 'Can you run?'

'Sure I can run,' said the freshman, and he shot away to cover a hundred metres in just over ten seconds.

'Great!' said the coach. 'But can you pass a ball?'

'Well,' replied the freshman hesitantly, 'I guess if I can swallow it, I can probably pass it.'

Baseball

One day, the Devil challenged God to a baseball game between Hell and Heaven.

'You don't have a chance,' said God. 'I have Babe Ruth, Mickey Mantle and all the greatest players up here.'

'Yes,' grinned the Devil, 'but I have all the umpires.'

What's the difference between a New York Yankees fan and a dentist?
– One roots for the yanks, the other yanks for the roots.

Reading through a magazine, a woman suddenly started laughing. Turning to her husband, she said: 'There's a classified ad here where a guy is offering to swap his wife for a season ticket to the Yankees. You wouldn't swap me for a season ticket, would you?'

'Of course not, honey,' replied the husband. 'The season's half over.'

A baseball team manager who had an ulcer visited his doctor.

The doctor advised: 'You have to remember not to get too excited. Don't get so worked up, and try to forget all about baseball when you're off the field. After all, it's only a game. By the way, how come you let the pitcher bat yesterday with the tying run on second and two men out in the ninth?'

Golf

A golfer put his tee shot at the first hole deep into a wood, but reckoned there was sufficient gap through the trees for him to get back on to the fairway with his second shot. But he miscalculated, and the ball smashed into a tree, rebounded onto his forehead and killed him.

As the man approached the gates of Heaven, golf club in hand, St Peter saw him and called out: 'Were you a good golfer?'

The golfer replied: 'Well, I got here in two, didn't I?'

Two strangers, John and Jerry, had paired up for a round of golf, but the afternoon was being spoiled by the slow play of two women in front. On the twelfth hole, John had suffered enough and marched towards the women to ask whether they would let him and his partner play through. He got halfway there and suddenly turned back.

'I'm sorry,' he explained to Jerry, 'but when I got closer, I realized that one of those women is my wife and the other is my mistress. Will you go and talk to them instead?'

So Jerry walked towards the two women. But

then he, too, stopped halfway before turning back.

'What's the problem?' asked John.

Jerry said: 'It's a small world . . .'

A golfer was lining up his shot when a voice from the clubhouse called out: 'Would the gentleman on the ladies' tee please move back to the men's tee!'

The golfer ignored the request and continued with his practice swings. The voice called out again: 'Sir, will you please move back to the men's tee now!'

The golfer carried on regardless and was just addressing the ball when the voice called out for a third time: 'This is your final warning! Move back to the men's tee immediately or I will have you thrown off the course.'

The golfer turned angrily in the direction of the clubhouse and shouted back: 'Do you mind being quiet while I play my second shot!'

As Tom and Ted set off for their weekly round of golf, Tom suggested: 'To add a bit of interest, let's have a bet of twenty dollars on the game.'

Ted agreed, and they enjoyed a close-fought match. With one hole to play, Tom led by a single stroke, but then on the eighteenth he hooked his ball into the rough.

'Help me find my ball,' he called to Ted. 'You search over there, I'll look around here.'

After five minutes of fruitless searching, Tom, knowing that he was facing a disastrous penalty for a lost ball, sneakily pulled a ball from his pocket, dropped it on the ground and called out triumphantly: 'Hey, I've found my ball!'

Ted looked across at him in disgust. 'After all the years we've been friends,' he said, 'how could you cheat on me at golf for a measly few bucks?'

'What do you mean – cheat?' protested Tom. 'I found my ball sitting right there!'

'And a liar, too!' exclaimed Ted in disbelief.

'What makes you think I'm lying?' yelled Tom.

'Because', said Ted, 'I've been standing on your ball for the last five minutes!'

After a terrible round, a golfer reached the eighteenth hole and spotted a lake beside the fairway. In despair he said to his caddie: 'I've played so badly today, I'm going to drown myself in that lake!'

The caddie gave him a withering glare and said: 'Do you think you'll be able to keep your head down that long?'

Why Golf Is Better Than Sex

A below par performance is considered good.

You can still make money doing it as a senior.

You can stop in the middle and have a couple of beers.

Three times a day is possible.

If your equipment gets old and rusty, you can replace it.

You don't have to cuddle your partner when you're finished.

You get to play a different hole every fifteen minutes.

Foursomes are encouraged.

A golfer was about to tee off when a beautiful naked lady ran past him. Although the incident distracted him somewhat, being a committed golfer he resumed his stance and addressed the ball once more. However, just as he was about to hit the shot, two men in white coats ran past him. He scratched his head in bewilderment . . . just as a third man in a white coat ran past him, carrying two buckets of sand.

Finally he was able to drive off and headed down the fairway, where he asked his playing partner if he had any idea what had been going on.

His companion said: 'Well, once a week that lady manages to escape from the mental hospital next to the course, tears off her clothes, and runs across the fairways. The three guys you saw were the nurses. They have a race to see who can catch her first, and the winner gets to carry her back.'

'What about the buckets of sand?'

'Well, that guy won last week; the buckets of sand are his handicap.'

A man who was a keen golfer phoned the doctor. 'Doctor, come quick, this is an emergency! My young son has swallowed my golf tees!'

'Okay,' said the doctor, 'I'll be with you as soon as I can.'

'Tell me what to do till you get here.'

The doctor said: 'Practise your putting.'

A ladies' golfing foursome was about to tee off when a male streaker suddenly emerged from some bushes and ran across the fairway.

One lady gasped: 'I think I know him. Isn't that Dick Green?'

'No,' said another. 'I think it's a reflection of the grass.'

A twenty-four-handicap golfer played the same course every week, and whenever he arrived at the par three eleventh hole, where the tee shot was over a lake, he took out an old ball because he invariably drove it into the water.

One night before his regular Friday round he had a vivid dream in which a booming voice told him he would birdie the eleventh the following day.

The next day he played his usual game, but when he stepped on to the eleventh tee, a voice boomed: 'Take out a new ball.'

Remembering the dream, he excitedly took out a brand new ball from his golf bag. 'Now take a practice swing,' boomed the voice.

So he took a practice swing.

And the voice boomed: 'Put back the old ball.'

Horse Racing

A man owned a racehorse that had never won a race. Finally the owner lost patience and warned the horse: 'Either you win this afternoon or you'll be pulling a milk cart tomorrow morning.'

That afternoon, the horse was lined up with the others in the starting gate. As the stalls opened, the rest of the field raced away, but as the gate was removed, the owner saw his horse fast asleep on the track.

Angrily he ran over, kicked the horse and yelled: 'Why are you sleeping?'

The horse wearily lifted its head and replied: 'I have to get up at half past three in the morning.'

A horse was leading by ten lengths in the Derby with just two furlongs to go. Then suddenly the jockey was hit by a barrage of sausage rolls and pork pies. He managed to keep control of the horse, only to be struck by a dish of smoked salmon and several chicken drumsticks. He still had the horse just in front inside the final furlong until a blow on the head from a bottle of Chardonnay and a chocolate cake saw him relinquish the lead and finish only second. The angry jockey marched straight to the stewards to complain that he'd been hampered.

Soccer

A soccer goalkeeper was walking along the street one day when he heard screams coming from an apartment block. He looked up to see smoke billowing from a fifth-floor window and a woman leaning out holding her baby.

'Help! Help!' cried the woman. 'I need someone to catch my baby.'

A crowd of onlookers had assembled, but nobody was confident about catching a baby dropped from such a great height. Then the goalkeeper stepped forward. 'I'm a professional goalkeeper,' he called to the woman. 'I'm famous for my safe hands. Drop the baby and I promise I will catch it. For me, it will just be like catching a ball.'

The woman agreed and shouted back: 'Okay. When I drop my baby, treat it as if you were catching a ball.'

On a count of three, the woman dropped the baby. Everyone held their breath as the goalkeeper positioned himself to catch it. There was a huge sigh of relief, followed by wild cheering, as the goalkeeper caught the baby safely in his arms. Then he bounced it twice on the ground and kicked it fifty yards down the street.

A man who had been a Chelsea fan all his life suddenly switched his allegiance to Crystal Palace.

'Why have you started watching Crystal Palace?' asked his neighbour.

The man said: 'My doctor said I should avoid excitement.'

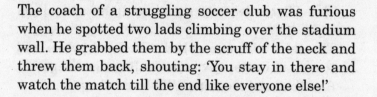

The coach of a struggling soccer club was furious when he spotted two lads climbing over the stadium wall. He grabbed them by the scruff of the neck and threw them back, shouting: 'You stay in there and watch the match till the end like everyone else!'

A man went into a barber's shop that advertised David Beckham-style haircuts. Fifteen minutes later, he glanced in the mirror and saw his scalp erratically shaven and his head covered in cuts.

The man protested: 'That's not how David Beckham has his hair!'

The barber said: 'It would be if he came here.'

Three elderly soccer fans were in a church praying. The first one asked: 'Oh Lord, when will England next win the World Cup?'

And the Lord replied: 'In eleven years' time.'

'But I'll be dead by then,' said the first old man.

The second old man asked: 'Oh Lord, when will Manchester City win the Champions League?'

And the Lord replied: 'In fifteen years' time.'

'But I'll be dead by then,' said the second old man.

The third old man asked: 'Oh Lord, when will Nottingham Forest next win the Premier League?'

And the Lord answered: 'I'll be dead by then!'

The Seven Dwarfs got trapped in a mineshaft. Snow White ran to the entrance and shouted down to them. From the dark depths a voice called back: 'Scotland will win the 2014 World Cup.'

Snow White breathed a sigh of relief. 'Thank God,' she said. 'At least we know Dopey's still alive!'

Travel

A man went to a travel agent to book his summer holiday. He told the travel agent: 'Last year you sold me a holiday to Mauritius and my wife got pregnant. The year before you sold me a holiday to the Bahamas and my wife got pregnant again. And the year before that it was Florida and my wife got pregnant then, too.'

'I see,' said the travel agent. 'Where did you have in mind this year?'

'Somewhere cheaper,' said the man, 'so that she can come with me for once.'

As part of its random testing programme for pilots, the Federal Aviation Administration paid a pre-Christmas visit to Santa Claus. In preparation for what he knew would be a thorough examination of his flying skills, Santa had the elves wash the sled and bathe the reindeer. The examiner walked slowly around the sled, checking the reindeer harnesses and the landing gear. Satisfied that everything was in order, he told Santa it was time for the test ride.

Santa climbed into the sled, fastened his seat belt and checked his compass. Then the examiner jumped in, carrying, to Santa's surprise, a shotgun.

'What's that for?' asked Santa.

The examiner winked and whispered: 'I'm not really supposed to tell you this ahead of the test, but you're gonna lose an engine on takeoff.'

A man got lost and called in to a village shop to ask for directions. He asked the shopkeeper: 'Can you tell me the quickest way to Bristol?'

'Are you walking or driving?' asked the shopkeeper.

'Driving.'

'Good, because that's definitely the quickest way.'

A man, a pig and a dog were the sole survivors of a terrible shipwreck. They found themselves stranded on a desert island where they soon developed a routine of going to the beach every evening to watch the sun go down.

One particular evening, the sky was red with beautiful wispy clouds and the breeze was warm and gentle. It was a perfect night for romance. As the three of them sat there, the pig began to look increasingly attractive to the man. After a while, he leaned over to the pig and put his arm around it. But the dog was instantly jealous and growled menacingly until the man removed his arm from around the pig. After that, the three continued to enjoy the sunsets together but there was no more cuddling.

Two months later, there was another shipwreck in the area and the only survivor was the most beautiful young woman the man had ever seen. She was in a bad way when she was washed up on their island but slowly he nursed her back to health until she was well enough to join the three of them on the beach for their sunset ritual. It was another beautiful evening – red sky, wispy clouds, a warm, gentle breeze, perfect for romance. Pretty soon, the man started to get those urges again. He fought them as long as he could but eventually he could contain himself no longer. So he leaned over to the beautiful young woman and whispered in her ear: 'Would you mind taking the dog for a walk?'

With the car hood up, a man was carrying out repairs to the vehicle's engine. A tramp came along and looked to see what the man was doing.

The man explained: 'Piston broke.'

'Me, too,' sighed the tramp wearily.

A woman was driving along the road when the car in front braked suddenly and she ploughed into the back of it.

When the driver got out, the woman saw that he was short of stature. He said: 'I'm not happy.'

The woman said: 'Well, which one ARE you?'

A man and a woman were sitting next to each other in the first-class section of an aeroplane. After a few minutes, the woman sneezed, took a tissue, gently wiped her nose and shuddered violently in her seat.

Mystified by the shuddering, the man nevertheless continued reading his book. But a few minutes later the same thing happened again. The woman sneezed, took a tissue, gently wiped her nose and shuddered violently in her seat.

The man was becoming increasingly curious about the shuddering and, sure enough, a few minutes later, it happened again. The woman sneezed, took a tissue, gently wiped her nose and shuddered violently in her seat.

This time the man could remain silent no longer. 'Excuse me,' he said, 'but three times you have sneezed, taken a tissue, wiped your nose and then shuddered violently. What's it all about?'

'I'm sorry,' said the woman, 'but I suffer from a rare condition. Every time I sneeze, I have an orgasm.'

'Oh dear,' said the man, now feeling acutely embarrassed. 'I've never heard of that condition before. What are you taking for it?'

The woman looked at him and said: 'Pepper.'

An elderly man went to a train station booking office and said: 'I'd like a return ticket, please.'

'Where to?' said the clerk.

'Back to here, of course,' said the old man.

A luxury cruise ship sailing in the Pacific sank in a tropical storm. Among the few survivors was a young man who managed to swim through the shark-infested waters to reach a remote desert island. As he lay exhausted on the beach, he noticed another figure a few hundred years away. It was a woman who had been washed ashore from the same ship. She was in a bad way, but he managed to administer mouth-to-mouth resuscitation and brought her back to life. As he stepped back, he realized that the woman was Elle Macpherson.

Elle was so grateful to the young man for saving her life that they set up home together on the deserted island and made love three times a day. For months they led an idyllic existence, untroubled by other members of the human race, until one day Elle noticed that her lover appeared rather sad.

'What's the matter, darling?' she asked. 'You look so sad. Is there anything I can do to help?'

'Yes, there is actually,' replied the young man. 'Elle, would you mind putting on my shirt?'

'Sure. Anything for you.'

'Now would you put on my pants?'

'No problem if it makes you feel better.'

'Now would you put on my hat?'

'Your wish is my command.'

'And would you mind if I drew a little moustache on your face?'

'Whatever you want, darling.'

'Now will you start walking around the edge of the island?'

Dressed in his clothes and with a moustache drawn on her top lip, Elle Macpherson started walking around the perimeter of the island while he set off in the opposite direction. When they met halfway round, he rushed up to her excitedly and yelled: 'Dude! You'll never guess who I'm sleeping with!'

After her car had leaked oil all over her driveway, a woman went to her local pet shop to buy an extra-large bag of cat litter to soak it up. It proved so successful that an hour later she went back to the pet shop and bought another extra-large bag of cat litter to finish the job.

The sales clerk remembered her. He looked thoughtfully at her purchase and said: 'Lady, if that were my cat, I'd put him outside!'

At the airport check-in desk, a woman passenger told the clerk: 'I want you to send one of my bags to New York, one to Chicago and the other one to Los Angeles.'

'Sorry, we can't do that,' said the clerk.

The woman snapped: 'Well, you did last week!'

During his lunch break at work, a man received a phone call from his wife, asking him to pick up some groceries on his way home. Reminding her that this was his golf league afternoon, he said he would be happy to go to the store after his round of golf.

After playing his round, he stopped at the store and collected two bags of groceries. He then carried the bags to his Rolls-Royce in the car park, but when he got to the car he struggled to reach into his pocket for his keys because his arms were full.

Seeing a pretty young woman walking past, he called out to her: 'Excuse me, could you help me? I can't reach into my pocket to get my car keys out so that I can open the door and put these groceries away. Do you think you could reach into my pocket for my keys?'

'Sure,' she said.

So she pulled the keys out of his pocket but with them came two golf tees, which fell to the ground.

'What are these for?' she asked.

'Oh,' he replied, 'those are to keep my balls in the air while I'm driving.'

'Gee!' she exclaimed. 'Those Rolls-Royce people think of everything!'

On an aeroplane, what is the difference between a good landing and a great landing?
– A good landing is one where everyone on board is able to walk away; a great landing is one where the plane can be used again.

A wealthy lady was being driven around by her chauffeur when their limo got a flat tyre.

He got out and started trying to prise off the hubcap, but was struggling to shift it.

After a few minutes, the lady leaned out of the window and said: 'Would you like a screwdriver?'

'We might as well,' he replied, 'because I can't get this bloody wheel off.'

A budget airline flight was delayed for nearly two hours. When the plane finally took off, the passengers asked the flight attendant the reason for the late departure.

'Well,' she explained, 'the pilot was worried about a noise he heard coming from one of the engines, and it took us a while to get a new pilot.'

The navigator of a luxury cruise liner was steering the ship through dense fog. After a while, he turned to the captain and said: 'Sir, I think something is wrong with our compass.'

'What makes you think that?' asked the captain.

'Because', said the navigator, 'we've just been overtaken by a number 42 bus.'

On a crowded commuter train in rush hour, a middle-aged woman found herself pressed up against a male passenger. As the train rocked from side to side, their bodies repeatedly made contact. His presence made her extremely uncomfortable until finally she turned to him and said: 'If you don't stop poking me with your thing, I'm calling the police.'

'I don't know what you mean,' said the man. 'It's just my wages packet in my pocket.'

'Well, you must have a good job,' she scoffed, 'because that's the fifth raise you've had in the last twenty minutes!'

A pilot and co-pilot were in a light aircraft that was spinning dangerously out of control. Starting to panic, the co-pilot said: 'If it carries on like this, do you think we'll fall out?'

'Of course not,' replied the pilot. 'We've been friends for years.'

A motorist took his car into a garage. 'Could you check the battery?' he asked the mechanic. 'I think it's flat.'

'Why?' said the mechanic. 'What shape did you want it to be?'

A young man asked his father, a church minister, if he could borrow the family car.

'Not until you get your hair cut,' said the father.

'What's your problem?' asked the son. 'Moses had long hair, so did Samson and even Jesus.'

'That's true,' said the father. 'And they also walked everywhere.'

How do you know if an airline pilot is at your party?
– He'll tell you.

When her car broke down, a woman called out a local mechanic to repair it. He lifted up the hood, looked in the engine, whacked something with a hammer and said: 'Try it now.'

To her amazement, the car started straight away.

'That's incredible,' she said. 'You've been here less than a minute and you've managed to fix it. I'm so grateful.'

'All part of the job, ma'am. That'll be two hundred and fifty dollars.'

The smile disappeared from the woman's face. 'How much?' she asked incredulously. 'How can you charge two hundred and fifty dollars when all you did was hit it with a hammer?'

'I can write you out an itemized bill if you like,' he suggested.

'Yes please,' she said firmly.

So he wrote out the bill and handed it to her. It read: 'Hitting engine with hammer – ten dollars. Knowing where to hit it – two hundred and forty dollars.'

When a bus driver pulled up at a bus stop, a giant of a man climbed on board and announced, 'Big John doesn't pay' before walking defiantly to a seat. Being on the skinny side, the driver thought better of getting into an argument with the passenger.

The same thing happened the following day. The man mountain got on the bus, glared at the driver and roared: 'Big John doesn't pay.' He then went straight to a seat.

This went on for several days, by the end of which the driver was beginning to resent Big John's attitude. He became determined to make Big John pay the fare just like everyone else and to that end, enrolled on a three-week bodybuilding course at the local gym.

Now with rippling muscles where there had previously been skin and bone, the driver eagerly awaited his next confrontation with Big John. Sure enough at his usual stop, the huge passenger got on and declared: 'Big John doesn't pay.'

But this time the driver wasn't going to take it lying down. He rose to his feet, looked the passenger squarely in the eye and demanded: 'And why doesn't Big John pay?'

The passenger reached into his inside pocket. The driver momentarily feared for his life. Then the passenger said: 'Because Big John got bus pass.'

An elderly lady phoned an airline office in New York and asked: 'How long does it take to fly to Miami?'

'Just a minute . . .' said the clerk.

'Thank you,' the old lady said and hung up.

Bill was driving along the street when he went through a red light.

'Watch what you're doing,' said George, his passenger. 'You'll have an accident.'

'Don't worry,' said Bill. 'My brother does it all the time.'

At the next intersection, Bill drove straight through another red light.

'Are you crazy?!' yelled George. 'You'll get us both killed!'

'It's okay,' said Bill calmly. 'My brother does it all the time.'

The next lights were green but this time Bill slammed on his brakes.

'What have you stopped for?' asked George.

Bill said: 'My brother might be coming the other way.'

A travel writer was checking out of a hotel when he noticed a Native American chief sitting in the lobby.

'Who's that?' the writer asked the hotel manager.

'Oh, that's Big Chief Forget Me Not. He's ninety-seven and has an amazing memory. He can remember every single detail of his life, right back to when he was just one year old.'

Intrigued, the writer went over to the chief and attempted to strike up a conversation. 'Hi there,' said the writer. 'I hear you have a fantastic memory. Can you tell me what you had for breakfast on your eighteenth birthday?'

'Eggs,' replied the chief simply.

With that, the travel writer bade him farewell and went on to recount the story to several people. As a matter of protocol, they advised him that the correct way to address a Native American chief was not 'Hi there' but 'How?'

A year later, the writer was staying at the same hotel and to his surprise Big Chief Forget Me Not was still sitting in the lobby.

So the writer went over to him and said: 'How?'

And the chief replied: 'Scrambled.'

While cruising at 35,000 feet, an aircraft suddenly shuddered violently. A passenger looked out of the window and exclaimed: 'My God! One of the engines just blew up!'

The passengers went white with fear, and moments later the aircraft was rocked by a second blast as the engine on the other side exploded.

The passengers started to panic, and even the flight attendants struggled to keep order. But just then the pilot strode confidently from the cockpit and assured everyone that there was nothing to worry about. Reassured by his air of supreme calm, the passengers returned to their seats as the pilot coolly walked to the door of the aircraft. There, he grabbed several packages from under the seats and handed them to the rest of the crew. The crewmembers quickly fastened the packages to their backs.

'Hey,' said an observant passenger. 'Aren't those parachutes?'

'Yes,' said the pilot.

'But I thought you said there was nothing to worry about?' asked the passenger.

'There isn't,' replied the pilot as a third engine exploded. 'We're going to get help.'

A man spotted a cheap cruise advertised in a travel agent's window. He went inside and handed over the ninety dollars for the cruise. Then the travel agent hit him over the head with a baseball bat and threw him in the river.

Shortly afterwards, another man was passing the travel agent's when he saw the same advert. He, too, went in and paid his ninety dollars. The travel agent then whacked him in the ribs with a baseball bat and threw him in the river.

As the two men, battered and bruised, floated down the river together, the first asked: 'Do you think they'll serve any food on the cruise?'

'I shouldn't think so,' said the second. 'They didn't last year.'

A train compartment contained three men and a beautiful young woman. As the four started talking, the young woman became increasingly flirtatious. Eventually she said: 'If each of you gives me five dollars, I'll show you my legs.'

The three men happily paid up, and the girl hitched up her dress to give them a good view of her legs. Then she said: 'If each of you gives me ten dollars, I'll show you my thighs.'

The men could hardly wait to reach for their wallets. They paid up, and the girl hitched her dress up even further to allow them to see her thighs.

Then she whispered: 'If each of you gives me fifty dollars, I'll show you where I was operated on for appendicitis.'

Salivating at the prospect, the men quickly handed over fifty dollars each. The girl then looked out of the window and pointed to a building they were passing.

'See there in the distance. That's the hospital where I had it done!'

A group of English tourists were travelling by coach around Ireland, but one woman did nothing but complain. She moaned about the hotels, the food, the weather, the people, the guides, everything. She was the tourist from Hell.

When the group arrived at the site of the famous Blarney Stone, the tour guide said: 'Legend has it that kissing the Blarney Stone will bring you good luck for the rest of your life. Unfortunately it's being cleaned today and so no one will be able to kiss it. Perhaps we can come back tomorrow.'

'We can't be here tomorrow,' moaned the miserable tourist. 'We have some other boring tour to go on. So I guess we can't kiss the stupid stone at all.'

'Well now,' said the guide, just about controlling his temper, 'it is also said that if you kiss someone who has kissed the stone, you'll have the same good fortune.'

'And I suppose you've kissed the stone?' sneered the woman.

'No, madam,' replied the guide. 'But I have sat on it!'

Working Life

One by one the managers of a company were called into the CEO's office until only the newest, most junior manager was left sitting nervously outside. Finally it was his turn to be summoned. He entered the office to find the CEO and the twelve senior managers seated solemnly around a table.

Addressing the junior manager, the CEO said: 'Young man, have you ever slept with Miss Henderson, our company secretary?'

'No, certainly not.'

'Are you absolutely sure?' the CEO persisted.

'Absolutely. I swear I've never laid a finger on her.'

'You'd swear that on the Bible?'

'Yes, I'd swear on the Bible that I've never had a sexual relationship with your secretary.'

'Good,' said the CEO. 'Then you can fire her.'

Why did the mathematician turn off the heating in his home?
– So he could be cold and calculating.

A businessman told his neighbour that his company was looking for a new accountant.

'Didn't your company hire a new accountant a few weeks ago?' asked the neighbour.

'Yes,' said the businessman. 'That's the accountant we're looking for.'

How do you know when an accountant is on vacation?
– He doesn't wear a tie to work and comes in at 8.31.

When does a person decide to become an accountant?

– When he realizes he doesn't have the charisma to succeed as an undertaker.

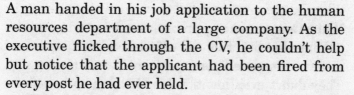

A man handed in his job application to the human resources department of a large company. As the executive flicked through the CV, he couldn't help but notice that the applicant had been fired from every post he had ever held.

'This CV isn't much of a recommendation,' said the HR executive. 'You've been fired from every job. Can you name one positive aspect to such a terrible employment record?'

The man thought for a moment and said: 'Well, at least it shows I'm not a quitter!'

A young man complained to his friend: 'I was sacked from my new job today for asking the customers if they wanted "Smoking or Non-Smoking".'

'That's a bit harsh,' said the friend.

'I thought so, too. But the funeral director told me the correct phrase was "Cremation or Burial".'

A man came home and told his wife: 'I got fired at work today. My boss said my communication skills were awful.'

'What did you say?'

'I didn't know what to say.'

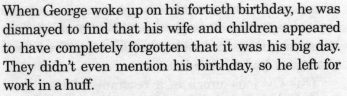

When George woke up on his fortieth birthday, he was dismayed to find that his wife and children appeared to have completely forgotten that it was his big day. They didn't even mention his birthday, so he left for work in a huff.

When he arrived at the office, his pretty secretary Rachel immediately wished him Happy Birthday.

'Thank you, Rachel,' said George. 'That's the nicest thing that's happened to me all day. You're the only person who seems to have remembered.'

Later in the morning, Rachel asked George if he fancied going out for lunch by way of celebration.

'Yes, why not?' he said. 'After all, it is my birthday.'

So the two of them dined in a cosy restaurant and after a couple of glasses of wine, she turned to him and said: 'My apartment is just around the corner. Would you like to see it?'

'Sure,' replied George.

Arriving at her apartment, George sat on the couch while Rachel went into the bedroom, promising that she would be right back. A couple of minutes later, she reappeared, followed by George's family, friends and co-workers.

George just sat there . . . naked.

The CEO of a major international company was due to speak to a key convention, so he asked Jones, one of his minions, to write him a dynamic, twenty-minute speech. But when the CEO returned from the event, he was fuming.

'Why the hell did you write me a one-hour speech?' he raged. 'Half the audience began to walk out long before I was finished!'

Jones was puzzled. 'I did write you a twenty-minute speech, sir,' he said. 'I also gave you the two extra copies you asked for.'

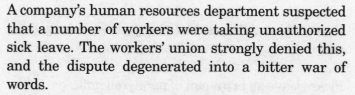

A company's human resources department suspected that a number of workers were taking unauthorized sick leave. The workers' union strongly denied this, and the dispute degenerated into a bitter war of words.

Then one day, the HR director marched in to the union leader's office brandishing a newspaper.

Pointing to a photograph on the back page, the HR director raged: 'This man called in sick yesterday but here on the sports page is a picture of him winning a local golf tournament with a score of two under par!'

The union leader glanced at the picture, tossed the paper aside and said: 'Well, just think of the score he could have made if he hadn't been sick!'

A man owned a dog that howled all night, every night. Eventually the man concluded that the dog had too much testosterone, so he took the animal to the vet to be castrated. But to the despair of the man and his neighbours, the dog continued howling.

Finally he said to the dog: 'You've had the operation. Why are you still howling?'

The dog replied: 'Because now I'm a consultant.'

Genuine Notes to Milkmen

Dear milkman, I've just had a baby, please leave another one.

Please leave an extra pint of paralysed milk.

Milkman, please could I have a loaf but no bread today.

Sorry not to have paid your bill before, but my wife had a baby and I've been carrying it around in my pocket for weeks.

Please send me details about cheap milk as I am stagnant.

Milk is needed for the baby. Father is unable to supply it.

My daughter says she wants a milkshake. Do you do it before you deliver or do I have to shake the bottle?

Please send me a form for cheap milk, for I have a baby two months old and did not know about it until a neighbour told me.

Please leave no milk today. When I say today, I mean tomorrow, for I wrote this note yesterday.

Milkman, please close the gate behind you because the birds keep pecking the tops off the milk.

When you leave the milk, please put the coal on the boiler, let dog out and put newspaper inside the screen door. PS Don't leave any milk.

The chickens in a large hen house started to fight, and a number died of their injuries every day. So the farmer sought the advice of a rural affairs consultant.

'Add baking powder to the chickens' food,' suggested the consultant. 'It will calm them down.'

A week later, the farmer returned to the consultant and said: 'My chickens are still dying. Is there anything else I can try?'

'Add strawberry juice to their drinking water,' said the consultant. 'That will help for sure.'

Three days later, the farmer went back to the consultant. 'It's no good. My chickens are still fighting. Do you have any more advice?'

'I can give you more and more advice,' answered the consultant. 'The real question is whether you have more chickens.'

A worker went up to his employer, showed him his last wage packet and said: 'This is two hundred dollars short.'

'I know,' said the employer. 'But last week I overpaid you two hundred dollars, and you didn't say anything then.'

'Well,' said the worker, 'I don't mind the occasional mistake, but when it becomes a habit, I feel I have to draw it to your attention.'

A man attending a job interview was asked what he thought his greatest qualities were.

'My motivational skills,' he replied. 'At my last job everyone said they had to work twice as hard when I was around.'

A lowly office worker named Eric boasted to his boss that he knew every famous person in the world, including celebrities, royalty and heads of state. Not surprisingly, his boss scoffed at the claim, so Eric promised to introduce him to some of his famous friends.

'Would you believe me', asked Eric, 'if I took you to meet Arnold Schwarzenegger?'

'Maybe,' said the boss.

So they drove to Schwarzenegger's mansion, and Arnie came to the door to greet them. 'Hey, Eric, how you doin'? Long time no see. Why don't you and your friend come in for lunch?'

They stayed for two hours, eating and drinking at Arnie's expense. As they left, Eric said to his boss: 'Now are you convinced?'

'You just got lucky,' said the boss with a sneer. 'Arnie's a naturally friendly guy.'

'Okay,' sighed Eric. 'What if I introduced you to Madonna? Then would you believe that I know everybody worth knowing?'

'Hmm, perhaps,' conceded the boss.

So they flew to London, where Eric took his boss to Madonna's house.

'Eric, great to see you again,' said Madonna. 'Who's your friend?'

'This is my boss,' said Eric.

'Come in, both of you. Any friend of Eric's is a friend of mine.'

An hour later, they left and Eric asked his boss: 'Now do you believe me?'

'I don't know,' said his boss. 'You could have tipped her off in advance and paid her to say she knew you.'

Eric shook his head in despair, and then said: 'How about if I showed you I was friends with the Pope?'

'I guess that would be pretty impressive,' said the boss. 'If you could get to stand on the Vatican balcony with the Pope, then yes I'd finally be convinced that you know every famous person in the world.'

So the pair travelled to Rome. The boss waited in St Peter's Square while Eric entered the Vatican. A few minutes later, true to his word, Eric appeared on the Vatican balcony alongside the Pope.

Immediately afterwards, Eric rushed back down to the square to find his boss's reaction, only to discover that he had fainted.

'What happened?' asked Eric.

'I was fine,' said the boss wearily, 'until the guy next to me said: "Who's that on the balcony with Eric?"'

George came home from work, ate his dinner and slumped in the chair. Worried that he was working too hard and needed to relax, his wife went over to him and started caressing him tenderly.

'Get off, woman,' he said testily. 'I get enough of that at the office!'

On a baking hot summer's day, the temperature in the open plan office was nudging ninety degrees and the foul stench of perspiration was coming from one desk in the corner.

Eventually one of the workers said pointedly: 'Obviously someone's deodorant isn't working.'

The guy at the desk in the corner called back: 'Well, it can't be me because I'm not wearing any.'

Why did the man quit his job at the helium gas factory?
– Because he didn't like being spoken to in that tone of voice.

What Advertising Terms Really Mean

NEW: Different colour from previous design.

ALL NEW: Parts are not interchangeable with previous design.

REDESIGNED: Previous flaws fixed – we hope.

EXCLUSIVE: Imported product.

UNRIVALLED: Almost as good as the competition.

ENERGY SAVING: When the power is off.

ADVANCED DESIGN: The advertising agency doesn't understand it.

FUTURISTIC: No other reason why it looks the way it does.

LATEST AEROSPACE TECHNOLOGY: One of our tech guys was laid off by Boeing.

FIELD TESTED: Manufacturer lacks proper testing equipment.

YEARS OF DEVELOPMENT: We finally got one to work.

BREAKTHROUGH: We finally figured out a use for it.

FOOLPROOF OPERATION: No provision for adjustments.

PERFORMANCE PROVEN: Will operate through the warranty period.

DIRECT SALES ONLY: Factory had a major argument with distributor.

MAINTENANCE FREE: Impossible to repair.

MEETS ALL STANDARDS: Ours, not yours.